Reading Games

Jackie Silberg

Other books by Jackie Silberg:

125 Brain Games for Babies: Simple Games to Promote Early Brain Development

125 Brain Games for Toddlers and Twos: Simple Games to Promote Early Brain Development

300 Three Minute Games: Quick and Easy Activities for 2-5 Year Olds

500 Five Minute Games: Quick and Easy Activities for 3-6 Year Olds

All About Me

Brain Games for Babies, Toddlers, and Twos: 140 Fun Ways to Boost Development

The Complete Book of Activities, Games, Stories, Props, Recipes, and Dances for Young Children: Over 600 Selections

The Complete Book of Rhymes, Songs, Poems, Fingerplays, and Chants: Over 700 Selections

Games to Play With Babies, Third Edition

Games to Play With Toddlers, Revised

Games to Play With Two-Year-Olds, Revised

Go Anywhere Games for Babies

Hello Rhythm: Rhythm Activities, Songs, and Games to Develop Skills

Hello Sound: Creative Music Activities for Parents and Teachers of Young Children

Higglety, Pigglety, Pop!: 233 Playful Rhymes and Chants

The I Can't Sing Book: For Grownups Who Can't Carry a Tune in a Paper Bag… But Want to Do Music With Young Children

I Live in Kansas

I Love Children Songbook

The Learning Power of Laughter

Let's Be Friends

Lollipops and Spaghetti Activity Book: Developmental Activities

My Toes Are Starting to Wiggle and Other Easy Songs for Circle Time

Peanut Butter, Tarzan, and Roosters Activity Book

Sing Yeladim

Sniggles, Squirrels, and Chickenpox: 40 Original Songs With Activities for Early Childhood

Songs to Sing With Babies

Reading Games

for Young Children

Jackie Silberg

Illustrated by Deborah C. Wright

gryphon house

Beltsville, MD

Acknowledgments

With my sincerest appreciation, I want to thank Larry Rood and Leah Curry-Rood of Gryphon House and Kathy Charner, my editor, for all of the support, interest, encouragement, and caring that they give to me. We all benefit in the name of young children.

Dedication

I dedicate this book to the alphabet.

Copyright

© 2005 Jackie Silberg
Published by Gryphon House, Inc.
10726 Tucker Street, Beltsville, MD 20705
800.638.0928; 301.595.9500; 301.595.0051 (fax)

Visit us on the web at www.gryphonhouse.com

The author of this book, Jackie Silberg, is an acclaimed speaker, teacher, and trainer on early childhood development and music. You can arrange to have her speak, present, train, or entertain by contacting her through Gryphon House, PO Box 207, Beltsville, MD 20704-0207, 800.638.0928, or at jsilberg@interserv.com.

Illustrations: Deborah C. Wright
Cover Photograph: Straight Shots

Library of Congress Cataloging-in-Publication

Silberg, Jackie, Date
  Reading games / by Jackie Silberg.
     p. cm.
  Includes bibliographical references and index.
  ISBN13: 978-0-87659-243-4
  ISBN10: 0-87659-243-4
  1. Reading games. 2. Reading (Early childhood) I. Title.
  LB1029.G3S55 2005
  372.41--dc22
                                            2004024125

Bulk purchase

Gryphon House books are available for special premiums and sales promotions as well as for fund-raising use. Special editions or book excerpts also can be created to specification. For details, contact the Director of Marketing at Gryphon House.

Disclaimer

Gryphon House, Inc. and the author cannot be held responsible for damage, mishap, or injury incurred during the use of or because of activities in this book. Appropriate and reasonable caution and adult supervision of children involved in activities and corresponding to the age and capability of each child involved, is recommended at all times. Do not leave children unattended at any time. Observe safety and caution at all times.

Table of Contents

Chapter 3 **Letter Sound Games**

Chapter 4 **Name Games**

Chapter 5 **Oral Blending and Segmenting Games**

Chapter 6 **Rhyming Games**

Chapter 7 **Sequencing Games**

Chapter 8 **Sight Word Games**

Chapter 9 **Story Play Games**

Chapter 10 **Word Games**

Chapter 11 **Writing Games**

Appendix

Index

Introduction

Learning to read: Everybody talks about it. Everybody thinks about it. Everyone has his or her own ideas about how to do it, what age to do it, what to do first. It's maddening! It's opinionated! It's frustrating! It's confusing! So how *do* you teach children to read? It's really quite simple: You teach children to read by talking, reading, and writing together every day, by making books a part of each day.

The list of what to do to teach children to read goes on and on—sing songs, learn rhymes, say poems, find words in an encyclopedia, tell stories, listen to what children say, make books together by writing the words and asking the children to draw pictures, and lots more, including the ideas in this book. Pick games from this book to build the important skills necessary for children to become successful readers. And when you do the games with children, they will discover that learning to read is fun and exciting.

What greater gift can you give a child than the gift of reading!

How to Use This Book

Each chapter in this book is full of fun and developmentally appropriate games that are necessary for learning to read, including games of alliteration, oral blending, writing, alphabet recognition, letter sounds, word play, and rhyming. These games will develop a love for language and joy of reading.

One way to use the games in this book is to pick and choose from each chapter. This strategy works because the games complement each other. For example, in the alliteration chapter when making up sentences with words that start with the same letter, go to the alphabet recognition chapter and follow up with a game uses that same letter again. Because each chapter contains a variety of games, they will suit the needs and abilities of many children.

Another way to use the material in the book is to concentrate on one chapter at a time. If this is the case, start with the alphabet chapter and follow it with the letter sounds chapter. Rhyming would come next, followed by names and oral blending. The rest of the chapters can really follow in any order that you choose. This order works best because children first need to recognize the letters of the alphabet by sight and sound in order to hear the phonemes. When they know the sounds, they will be able to hear rhymes and parts of words (segments).

Take your time with these games; repeat games that you and your beginning readers find enjoyable and successful.

The children of today are our future. They need to be highly literate and have critical thinking skills in order to compete in the 21st century.

About Reading and the Brain

Scientific research has shown the importance of touching, talking, smiling, and reading in the physical growth of a child's brain in the first few years of life. This exposure creates neural circuits and connections in the brain that are the basis for language and learning.

A dyslexia research team at Yale University's Center for Learning and Attention lead by Dr. Sally Shaywitz found a window on the brain through an imaging technique called functional MRI. These medical scientists identified parts of the brain used in reading. By observing the flow of oxygen-rich blood to working brain cells, they found that people who know how to sound out words can rapidly process what they see.

When fluent readers are asked to imagine the word "cat" without the "kah" sound, they readily summon up the word "at." The MRI photographs show their brains lighting up like pinball machines. When the brain gets it, the lightbulbs really do go on. However, the brains of people who can't sound out words often look different on MRI pictures. There is less blood flow to the language centers of the brain and, in some cases, not much activity evident at all. Scientists are not sure why this is or what it means. But simply put, without the ability to sound out words, the brain is stumped.

This research supports the idea that the brain learns to read the same way it learns to talk, one sound at a time. When babies first learn to talk they may slowly say one sound at a time. Once they get the hang of it, they speed up. Our brain becomes adept at processing and our experience is that of hearing words, but actually our brain is processing sounds (phonemes) and putting them together so we hear words. When we read, the same process is in operation. Our brain is processing one sound at a time but we perceive it as a whole word. For good readers, the process is so fast it appears that they are reading whole words, but, in fact, they are converting the letters on the written page into sounds. The brain then recognizes groups of sounds as words.

The important thing to remember is that reading is not automatic but must be learned. The reader must develop a conscious awareness that the letters on the page represent the sounds of the spoken word. To read the word "cat," the reader must parse, or segment, the word into its underlying phonological elements—/c/ /a/ /t/. Once the word is in its phonological form, it can be identified and understood.

What to Do to Help Children Learn to Read

The following are things you can do to encourage and inspire children as they learn to read and write.

With preschoolers, you can:
- Create reading rituals. Have a regular reading time every day.
- Read with expression. Emphasize rhythm and rhymes, and use different voices for characters.
- Visit the library often and participate in children's activities there.
- Sing songs, say nursery rhymes, and use sign language, if children know how.
- Give children materials to color, draw, and cut; do puzzles.
- Talk about everyday happenings. Explain what you're doing and how things work.
- Let children help with chores that include counting, sorting, measuring, and cooking.
- Play games that require following directions, listening, solving problems, and taking turns.
- Encourage children when they try to read and write.
- Be a good role model. Show children that reading is fun and important!

With kindergarteners, you can:
- Read out loud and talk about stories every day.
- Get library cards for children and go to the library regularly. Request songs and rhymes on tape.
- Read and say or sign nursery rhymes and sing songs together.
- Let them see you reading for fun.
- Have a writing supply box with crayons and paper.
- Listen to them. Ask them to listen to others.

With six-year-olds, you can:
- Play games with language to increase vocabulary, develop problem-solving skills, and practice letter sounds.

- Encourage children to ask questions about words.
- Talk about expressions and figures of speech to increase abstract thinking.
- Talk about challenging vocabulary words and concepts.
- Tell stories about real and imaginary events to increase comprehension.
- Listen to children read books aloud.

Why Is Reading With Children Important?

Reading to young children not only promotes language acquisition but also correlates with literacy development and, later on, with achievement in reading comprehension and overall success in school.

The percentage of young children who read aloud daily with a family member is one indicator of how well young children are prepared for school. Reading aloud:

- stimulates children's imagination,
- develops children's interest in reading and in books,
- improves children's listening skills,
- builds vocabulary,
- helps children to understand stories and "book language,"
- creates a bond between the reader and the child, and
- provides children with a positive role model.
  Source: *Family Reading*. NCES Fast Facts. National Center for Education Statistics, U.S. Department of Education.

The Five Essential Components of Reading

The Department of Education (July 2002) says that scientific research shows that there are five essential components of reading that children must be taught in order to learn to read. These five important elements in learning to read include the ability to:

1. hear the phonemes, or sounds, in words,
2. recognize words used often,
3. take apart words phonetically—phonics are important,
4. recognize the alphabet, and
5. make sense of what was read through discussion and rereading.

Alliteration Games

The use of alliteration (repetition of words starting with the same consonant or sound) is a relatively easy starting point to achieving phonemic awareness. Children develop phonemic awareness through exposure to literature and by doing informal activities that repeat or highlight sound patterns.

Drawing Alliteration

Teaches visualization

- Say an alliterative sentence, for example, "Bertha Bartholomew blew big, blue bubbles."
- Talk about drawing a picture about the sentence. What would be in the picture? Bertha and a big, blue bubble.
- Give children paper and drawing materials, and encourage them to create a picture.
- Help with the drawing, if necessary.
- Additional alliteration sentences that lend themselves to drawings are:
  - Floyd Flingle flipped flat flapjacks.
  - Lila Ledbetter lugged a lot of little lemons.
  - Randy Rathbone wrapped a rather rare red rabbit.

We Are Going to _____

Teaches vocabulary

- Say a sentence that starts, "We are going to the _____, and we will take a _____ and a _____."
- Each word in the blank spaces should start with the same letter. For example, "We are going to the **p**ark, and we will take a **p**iece of **p**aper and a **p**resent.
- Begin with only two words to fill in; add more words as vocabulary skills develop.
- With threes and fours, it's a good idea to describe how to play this game and talk about the vocabulary words before you use them.
- It is important to encourage children to repeat the words, so that they can hear and feel the sound.

Food Names

Teaches vocabulary

Group Game

- Sit in a circle.
- Ask the first child to say her name and then the name of a food that starts with the same letter. For example, "My name is Jackie and I like to eat jelly."
- Give each child a chance.
- Once everyone has created a sentence, start again and name two foods, then three, and so on.

The Alliteration Game

Teaches a sense of humor

- Choose a letter, for example, "B." Make the /b/ sound and practice saying words that start with the /b/ sound: "ball," "butter," "boy," and so on.
- Say words that all start with the letter. Put a group of words on paper large enough to see.
- After reading all of the words, try putting them together in a somewhat meaningful (or maybe silly!) way.
- The sillier the sentences get, the more fun you will have with the children.

Alan **a**te **a**nother **a**nteater.
Barry **b**ites **b**urger **b**uns.
Brother **B**ob **b**ounces **b**alls on his **b**ack.
But **B**etty **b**ites **b**ats **b**etter!
Carla **c**ut **c**auliflower, **c**arrots, and **c**ucumbers **c**arefully.
Catch the **c**razy **c**at-**c**ounting **c**raze!
Crafty **c**anyon-**c**reating **c**reatures **c**aught **c**rayfish.
Dinosaurs **d**ecorate **d**oughnuts in **D**enver.
Flying, **f**erocious **f**erns **f**oraging **f**or **f**ruit.
Frank **f**orgot to **f**ix the **f**aucet.
Justin's **j**eep **j**ust **j**umped, **j**oggled, and **j**iggled.
My **m**ommy **m**akes **m**arvelous, **m**unchy **m**eatballs.
Peggy **p**lans a **p**arty at the **p**ark.
Peter **P**iper **p**icked a **p**eck of **p**ickled **p**eppers.

- Make up a sentence and ask a child to raise her hand every time you say a word that starts with the /b/ sound.
- Make up several words that start with the same sound, using a child's name.

First Sound Fun

Teaches memory skills

Group Game

- Use alliteration to create an imaginative sentence.
- After you say the words, the children repeat them. For example:

> Adult: Mr. Martin makes
>
> Children: Mr. Martin makes
>
> Adult: Mr. Martin makes many mud pies.
>
> Children: Mr. Martin makes many mud pies.
>
> or
>
> Adult: Sister Sue says
>
> Children: Sister Sue says
>
> Adult: Sister Sue says sing songs.
>
> Children: Sister Sue says sing songs.

- Continue the game, making the sentences longer and longer.

The "B" Collection

Teaches cognitive skills

- This game is more meaningful if you have visited a museum or if children understand the concept of a collection. If not, explain that groups of similar items are called collections.
- Tell the children that you are going to create a "B" collection for friends and family to look at.
- Cover a small table with a white cloth. Gather items that start with the letter "B" to put on the table, such as a ball, baby picture, butter dish, book, and so on.
- Say, "Hello, this is the 'B' collection. It has a ball, book, butter dish…" (Say all the "B" items.).
- Repeat with other letters.

Acting Out Alliteration

Teaches dramatic play skills

Group Game

- Play "Aunt Abigail Asked Alice for an Apple."
- Choose a child to be Aunt Abigail and a child to be Alice. Give Alice an apple.
- Aunt Abigail says to Alice, "Hi Alice, I'm Aunt Abigail. May I have an apple?"
- Acting out words that start with the same sounds helps internalize the understanding of alliteration.
- Additional ideas include:
    - "Vicky Vine Viewed a Very Valuable Vase": select a child to be Vicky Vine and give her a vase to hold. Vicky says, "I'm Vicky Vine, and I am viewing a very valuable vase."
    - "Greta Gruber Grabbed a Group of Green Grapes": select a child to be Greta Gruber and give her some grapes. Greta says, "I'm Greta Gruber, and I grabbed a group of green grapes."

The First Sound Store

Teaches vocabulary

- Pretend to have a store that sells only things that begin with a certain sound.
- Once you have selected the sound, draw pictures of all of the words that you can think of that start with that sound. For example, have a store where everything starts with the /l/ sound, such as lilies, lights, lemons, lipsticks, and ladders.
- Discuss other possible sounds to use, and try them out in your store!

The Train Game

Teaches creativity

Group Game

- Pretend to be riding on a train.
- The children form a line by holding onto each other's waists.
- March around the room.
- Use alliteration to make up the name of a place where the train will stop. When you say the name of a place, the train stops and the children repeat the name.
- Say the name again and clap out the syllable(s). The children copy you.
- Some fun names are: bookie backie bok, sahara sahoola saloo, willy wally woo, jibber jabber jump.
- Follow up by imagining what the town looks like, who lives in the town, and what the people do in that town. This is a very imaginative game.

Willaby Wallaby Woo

Teaches listening skills

Group Game

- This popular song is wonderful for teaching alliteration. Here are the original words.

  Willaby Wallaby Woo
  An elephant stepped on you.
  Willaby Wallaby Wee
  An elephant stepped on me.

- Change the words to rhyme a child's name. For example, for the name Mary, the first two lines would change, and the rhyme would be:

  Willaby Wallaby Wary
  An elephant stepped on Mary.
  Willaby Wallaby Wee
  An elephant stepped on me.

Pawpaw Patch

Teaches rhythm

- The song "Pawpaw Patch" is wonderful for beginning alliteration practice.
- Say the words and accent the "p" words. Explain to the children that a pawpaw is a kind of fruit.

Where, oh where is pretty little Mary? (Repeat three times.)
*Way down yonder in the **P**aw**p**aw **P**atch.*
***P**icking up **P**aw**p**aws, **p**ut them in a basket* (Repeat three times.)
*Way down yonder in the **P**aw**p**aw **P**atch.*

- You can replace the "p" words with other letters. The letters "s", "t", and "m" are good to start with.

Betty, Batter, Butter, Bitter

Teaches dramatic play skills

Group Game

- This alliteration is fun to say and gives practice saying the /b/ sound.
- Before saying the rhyme, talk about the words "butter," "batter," and "bitter."
- Say the rhyme and accent the last word of each line.
- Encourage the children to say the words with you, especially the last word of each line.

> Betty bought a bit of **butter**,
> But said she this butter's **bitter**.
> If I put it in my **batter**,
> It will make my batter **bitter**.
> So Betty bought a bit of better **butter**,
> And put it in her **batter**,
> And made her batter **better**.

- This is also great to act out:

> *Betty goes to the store and buys the butter. She goes home and makes a cake. When she puts the butter in her batter, she tastes the batter and it is bitter. (Make a face for the bitter part.) She then goes back to the store and buys more butter that is better for her batter. End the drama with a picture of a beautiful cake.*

2

Alphabet Games

One of the best foundations for early reading success is familiarity with the letters of the alphabet. This skill is called letter recognition, one of the essential building blocks of reading. Build this familiarity by singing alphabet songs, matching pictures or objects with initial letters, or playing games with letters and sounds. Identifying letters and realizing that they represent the segments of speech is an important element in learning to read.

Texture Letters

Teaches creativity

- Trace and cut uppercase alphabet letters out of tag board, making the letters large.
- Encourage children to select materials to glue on the letter that starts with that letter, for example, for the letter "F," glue feathers on it. Or, for the letter "S" cover it with seeds.
- When the glue dries, the letters will become hard and the children will be able to feel the letters and trace them.

Letters in the Room

Teaches phonemic awareness and practice in writing letters

- You will need index cards, crayons, tape, and paper.
- Help children write the letters of the alphabet, putting one letter on each card.
- Walk around the room, naming the objects that you see, such as a table, chair, flower, goldfish, and so on.
- Starting with the table, ask a child to find the letter "T" index card and put it on the table. If you find more than one thing that begins with "T" then make more "T" index cards.

Writing on a Picture

Teaches following directions

- Draw a picture of a house. Include windows, a door, a chimney, and trees and flowers in the yard.
- Discuss the picture with a child so that he understands what everything is in the picture.
- Ask him to write the letter M in different places on the picture. For example, "Write an M on the window." or "Write an M on the door."
- Play this game with any letter of the alphabet.
- If the child cannot write the letter, use an alphabet stamp.

Write and Say

Teaches cognitive skills

- There are many ways to practice making letters.
- Choose one letter at a time.
- Write that letter in the air, on the floor with your foot or finger, on someone's back, on your head and on a piece of paper.
- Each time you write the letter, say its name.
- Do the same with every letter of your name.

The Alphabet Index

Teaches letter recognition

- You will need 26 index cards.
- Help the child write one letter of the alphabet on each card.
- Mix up the cards and ask the child to pick a card.
- Let him tell you the name of the letter and, if the child can, a word that begins with that letter.
- Now it's your turn to do the same.
- When you have finished naming 10 cards, stop the game. More than 10 may overload the child.

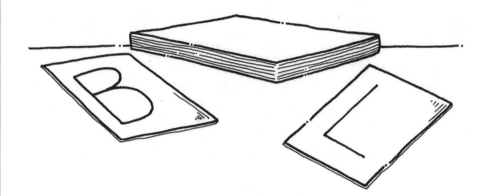

Bingo Art

Teaches following directions

- Children enjoy the song "Bingo." In addition to teaching sequencing, the song also teaches about letters.
- After singing the song, help a child write the letters "B," "I," "N," "G," and "O" on a piece of paper.
- Now draw a picture illustrating the song. Your picture can have a farmer, a dog, and the letters "B," "I," "N," "G," and "O" in it.
- Sing the song again and each time you say the letters "B," "I," "N," "G," and "O", point to them on the paper.

Rainbow Letters

Teaches about colors

- Write a large letter on a piece of paper.
- A child traces over the letter with four or more colors using crayons or markers. This makes a lovely rainbow letter.
- After doing this a few times, print the child's name using upper- and lowercase letters and let him turn the letters into rainbow letters.

Tracing Over Letters

Teaches fine motor skills

- This is a great way to help children learn the letters in the alphabet.
- Write letters on paper with glue.
- While the glue is still wet, sprinkle the letters with Jell-O powder.
- When these dry, they make great scratch-and-sniff letters to trace over.

Close Your Eyes Art

Teaches fine motor skills

- Drawing with your eyes closed takes a lot of cognitive thinking.
- You will need a large piece of drawing paper and crayons. Give a child a crayon and put his other hand on the paper so that he will know where it is.
- Ask him to close his eyes (or use a blindfold) and draw the beginning letter of his name. This may take several tries. The trying is all part of the fun.
- Once he has mastered a single letter, try another letter, and then, if appropriate, try an entire word.

Letter Games

Teaches observation skills

- Prepare a box with the letters of the alphabet on cards, one card for each letter.
- Ask a child to pick a card. He looks for a toy or some other item that begins with that letter.
- Using the same box of letters, ask a child to pick a card. Ask him to look through magazines and find five pictures that start with that letter.

Alphabet Art

Teaches vocabulary

Group Game

- You will need pieces of paper with a letter of the alphabet written on each piece, a container for the paper, and markers or crayons.
- Put the letters in the container and shake it up.
- Ask each child to select a letter without looking. When all of the children have picked a letter, they can look at their letters.
- The children write a word or draw a picture that begins with the letter they have chosen.
- After a few minutes, ask the children to share their word or picture with the rest of the group.

Find the Letter _

Teaches letter recognition

- You will need markers, paper, and alphabet flash cards.
- The child writes his name on a piece of paper with a marker.
- Show the alphabet flash cards one by one.
- When the child sees a flash card with one of the letters in his name, the child crosses it out on his paper with a marker.
- When all of the letters are crossed out, give the child a sticker.
- Another way to play the game is to use familiar words or sight words that the child is learning.

Feel the Letter

Teaches sensory perception

- Cut out some large letters from cardboard. Use letters that are meaningful to the child, such as beginning letters of family members' and pets' names.
- Put the letters in a box. A shoebox or an oatmeal box will work very well.
- Ask the child to close his eyes, or use a blindfold if the child is comfortable with one.
- The child picks a letter and tries to identify it by feeling the shape.

Where's the Letter?

Teaches creativity

- Write letters on index cards, one letter for each card. You can also use any pre-made materials with letters.
- Ask a child to pick a letter. He identifies the letter and then draws a picture of a word that begins with the letter.
- Then he writes the letter on the picture.
- This is great practice in recognizing letters and beginning sounds.

The Mail Is Here

Teaches vocabulary

Group Game

- Write a letter on small separate sheets of paper, one letter per sheet.
- Put each letter in a separate envelope and put the envelopes in a box.
- Say to the children, "The mail is here."
- Give an envelope to one child at a time.
- One by one, each child opens the envelope and says the name of the letter inside.
- All of the children look for objects in the room that start with that letter.
- They say the names out loud as you write them on a chalkboard or a white board.

Fill in the Letters

Teaches observation skills

- Write a string of letters of the alphabet. Leave out one letter and see if a child can fill in the missing letter. For example: A__CDE or GHIJK__MNOP.
- Say the letters out loud, skipping the missing letter.
- Ask the child to say the missing letter.

Looking for the "A"ce

Teaches observation skills

- Give the child a deck of playing cards.
- Show him what the Ace (the letter "A") looks like and then mix up the cards.
- As he turns over each card, say "no" to each card unless it is an Ace.
- For each ace, say "yes" and shout, "Hooray for the Ace!"
- Repeat, with you turning over the cards and the child saying "no" or "yes."

Card Royalty

Teaches observation skills

- Young children enjoy playing cards, and there are many good activities that use playing cards to teach numbers and letters.
- Take a deck of cards and pull out all of the Aces, Jacks, Queens, and Kings.
- Talk about the names of the cards and the first letters of the names of the cards.
- Mix up the Aces, Kings, Queens, and Jacks and, one by one, let a child turn over the cards.
- Starting with Aces, each time he discovers an Ace, you say with him, "Ace, Ace, where's your face? Hallelujah, here's an Ace!"
- Start again and look for Jacks. "Jack, Jack, break my back! Hallelujah, here's a Jack!" or "Queen Queen, you're so mean! Hallelujah, here's a Queen!" or "King, King, can you sing? Hallelujah, here's a King!"
- With each card that you look for, talk about the beginning letter and sound that it makes.

Alphabet Phone Conversation

Teaches cognitive skills

- Pretend to talk on the telephone with a child.
- The trick is that the only "words" that you can say are the letters of the alphabet in the correct order. For example, you start with "AAAA" and then the child says "BBBBB."
- Before beginning a phone conversation, talk about how you can say the letters with different kinds of expression. Make your voice go up or go down. Say part softly and part loudly. Also, try to make it sound like you are speaking to another person.
- You can also say more than one letter in your conversation. You could say, "AABBC," the child could say "DDE," and so on.
- This game is great fun and is wonderful alphabet practice.

Alphabet Singing

Teaches memory skills

- Sing the alphabet song with a child.
- Now sing it alone and stop after two or three letters. See if the child can fill in the next letter, for example, "ABCD_."
- If he gets the correct letter, continue on with the song and stop at another place.
- If he can't remember the letter, start at the beginning, sing the letter he missed, and stop right after that letter. You would sing "ABCDE_."
- This takes a lot of cognitive thinking and helps place letters in alphabetical order.

If Your Name...

Teaches the order of the alphabet

● Sing the following song to the tune of "If You're Happy and You Know It."

"If Your Name..." by Jackie Silberg

If your name starts with "A," clap your hands. (clap, clap)

If your name starts with "B," clap your hands. (clap, clap)

If your name starts with "C," or "D," or "E," you can jump up and down and clap your hands. (clap, clap)

If your name starts with "F," tap your foot. (tap, tap)

If your name starts with "G," tap your foot. (tap, tap)

If your name starts with "H," or "I," or "J," you can jump up and down and tap your foot. (tap, tap)

If your name starts with "K," blink your eyes. (blink, blink)

If your name starts with "L," blink your eyes. (blink, blink)

If your name starts with "M," or "N," or "O," you can jump up and down and blink your eyes. (blink, blink)

If your name starts with "P," shake your head. (shake, shake)

If your name starts with "Q," shake your head. (shake, shake)

If your name starts with "R," or "S," or "T," you can jump up and down and shake your head. (shake, shake)

If your name starts with "U," throw a kiss. (kiss, kiss)

If your name starts with "V," throw a kiss. (kiss, kiss)

If your name starts with "W," or "X," "Y," or "Z," you can jump up and down and throw a kiss! (kiss, kiss)

● Sing the song using just one letter, for example:

If your name begins with "B," stand up.

If your name begins with "B," stand up.

If your name begins with "B," and you're happy as can be,

If your name begins with "B," stand up.

Alphabet Camera

Teaches about using a camera

- Take pictures of things that start with "A" first, "B" next, "C", and so on. Try to take a few of each letter and take the pictures in alphabetical order.
- Ask the children to help you find the "right" picture.
- If the children are old enough, they might take the pictures themselves.
- Try to keep the pictures on the roll of film in alphabetical order. This will take several rolls of film.
- When the film is developed, put the pictures in a notebook in alphabetical order. It's best to have an "A" page, "B" page, and so on.

The Alphabet Activities

Teaches beginning letters of words

- Do activities every day with different letters.
- Write out the words for so the children can see and read them.
- Suggestions include:

Say your **a**ddress.

Eat an **a**pple.

Make the sound of your favorite **a**nimal.

Read a **b**ook.

Bounce a **b**all.

Ride your **b**icycle.

Count the trees in your yard.

Point to a **c**lock in your house.

Catch a ball.

Bark like a **d**og.

Quack like a **d**uck.

Wash the **d**ishes.

Walk like an **e**lephant.

Count to **e**leven.

Touch your **el**bow.

Hop like a **f**rog.

Jump **f**ourteen times.

Fly like a bird.

Wear the color **g**reen.

Jump like a **g**rasshopper.

Make someone **g**iggle.

Hop on one foot 10 times.

Gallop like a **h**orse.

Hug a friend.

Eat an **i**ce cream cone.

Look for an **i**cicle in cold weather.

Find a picture of an **i**nchworm.

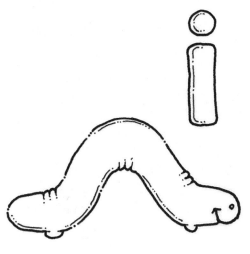

Tell someone a **j**oke.

Jog around the block with your mom.

Jump up and down five times.

Kick a ball.

Find a picture of a **k**angaroo.

Open a door with a **k**ey.

Hop on your **l**eft foot.

Write the **l**etters of your name.

Look at the **l**eaves on a tree.

Look at the **m**oon.

Jump like a **m**onkey.

Dance to your favorite **m**usic.

Write 10 **n**umbers.

Read the **n**ewspaper.

Go outside at **n**ighttime.

Open and close a door.

Eat an **o**range.

What's the **o**pposite of hello?

Paint a **p**retty **p**icture.

Color something **p**urple.

Count some **p**ennies.

Ask three **q**uestions.

Draw a **q**uilt pattern of squares and color each square.

Write your name as **q**uickly as you can.

Draw a **r**ainbow.

Draw two **r**ectangles.

Read your favorite book to someone.

Count the **s**tars in the sky.

Crawl like a **s**pider.

Cut **s**omething from a magazine with **s**cissors.

Move like a **t**urtle.

Tiptoe in the house.

Talk on the **t**elephone.

Use an **u**mbrella.

Look at a picture of a **u**nicorn.

Hide **u**nder a table.

Sing a song in a soft **v**oice.

Smell some **v**inegar.

Eat some **v**egetables.

Try to **w**histle.

Open a **w**indow.

Waddle like a duck.

Look at a picture of a **x**ylophone.

Draw a circle and put an "**X**" in the middle.

Draw a square and put an "**X**" in the middle.

Play with a **y**oyo.

Make a **y**ellow picture with crayons.

Yawn as if you are tired.

Make a **z**ero with your fingers.

Zip up a jacket.

Pretend to be an animal in the **z**oo.

● Make up your own ideas.

Outside the Window, I See _____

Teaches observation skills

- Look out the window and identify objects by the first letter in the name. For example, "Outside the window, I see something that begins with 'A.' it's an **a**pple tree."
- If possible, name things in alphabetical order—apple tree, bus, car, door, and so on.
- Or pick out a word or use the child's name and play the same game, using the order of the letters in the name as the guide. For example, for the name "Sam," you could use the words sign, ant, and mountain.

Name the Letter

Teaches letter recognition

Group Game

- On a large sheet of paper, print letters of all sizes and colors all over the paper.

Note: Be sure to print the letters right side up.

- Hang the paper on the wall.
- The children take turns coming to the paper, covering their eyes, and putting their index finger on the paper.
- Then they open their eyes and say name of the letter that their finger is on.
- If the children are a little older, they can also say a word that begins with that letter.

Circle the Letter

Teaches fine motor skills

- Write five different letters on a piece of paper. Make the letters large with room between each letter.
- Say one of the letters and ask a child to make a circle around the letter that you said.
- After you have finished with the first five letters, write five more letters on the paper.
- Reverse the procedure—ask a child to write the letters and you make the circles.

Eraser

Teaches cognitive skills

Group Game

- Write a series of 5-10 letters on a chalkboard or white board.
- Let one child at a time be "the eraser."
- Say a letter and ask the child to find and erase the correct letter.
- The child then passes the eraser to the next child.
- When all of the letters have been erased, start over.
- You can also play this game with familiar sight words that the children may recognize.

Making A's

Teaches creativity

- You will need craft sticks, glue, and cotton swabs.
- Show children how to make an "A" shape by placing two sticks in an upside-down V and then gluing on another stick across the middle of the V shape.
- Hold up the "A" stick and sing the following to the tune of "This Old Man":

    Here's an "A," here's an "A,"
    I have made an "A" today.
    With an "A," "A," "A," "A,"
    "A," "A," "A," "A," "A."
    I have made an "A" today.

- Walk around the room holding up the "A" and use it to touch everything you can find that starts with "A."

"A" Puppets

Teaches creativity

- Draw a large A on a piece of construction paper.
- Let children make a face on the A with a black marker.
- Tape or glue a craft stick on the back of the A to make a puppet.
- Hold the puppet and sing songs and talk about the letter "A." For example, "Hi, I'm the letter 'A' and I start lots of words, like 'apple,' 'apricot,' 'ape,' and 'acorn.'"
- Do this with every letter of the alphabet.

Giant Letters

Teaches motor skills

- Use colored masking tape to make a large letter on the floor. Choose a letter that you have been talking about.
- Suggest a variety of movements that a child could do on the letter, such as walk, march, hop, run, or crawl.
- Sing this song to the tune of "The Farmer in the Dell" as you move along the letter.

  I'm marching on the "F,"
  I'm marching on the "F,"
  Hi-ho, the derry-o,
  I'm marching on the "F."

- Continue singing the song as you hop on the "F," jump on the "F," and so on.

Body Alphabet

Teaches cognitive skills

Group Game

- Experiment with making letters with your body. The letter "T" is a good one to start with.
- Lay flat on your back and stretch your arms out to the side.
- Now try "S" Cognitively, this is a little more difficult because of the need to bend the body.
- Now make an "I," Lay flat on your back with your hands to the side.
- If you are playing this game with three children, you can now make the word "sit."
- Once you start this game, the children will try on their own to make other letters. It's a highly creative game.

The Parade of Letters

Teaches coordination

● Chant the following while marching around the room:

Here comes A.

Here comes B,

Marching along with letter C.

Right next to them, D and E,

Holding hands with F and G.

Next in line is H I J,

Waiting for the letter K.

L, M, N, O, and P,

Q, R, S, T, U and V

Are marching with W, X, Y, and Z.

Beat the drums,

Shout hooray,

The alphabet is here to stay!

10 Ways to Say the Alphabet

Teaches coordination

- For children who learn best by doing things with their bodies, try this game that focuses on moving and saying the alphabet.
- Say the alphabet:
  - to three people.
  - two times slowly and two times very fast.
  - while you jump up and down.
  - in a teeny tiny voice.
  - in a big roaring voice.
  - in a very slowly.
  - very, very fast.
  - with a clap in between each letter—"A" clap, "B" clap, and so on.
  - as you march around the room.
  - while standing on one foot.

Fill the Can

Teaches sharing

Group Game

- Decorate an empty coffee can.
- Write each child's name on a piece of paper, and put the names in a container.
- Draw one name and give that child the special can.
- The child finds objects to put in the can that start with the same letter as his name.
- Children can also take the can home and fill it with items from home that begin with the first letter of their name.

Find Your Letters

Teaches cognitive skills

- Print a child's name at the top of a piece of typing paper.
- Let him look around the room and find one thing that starts with each letter in his name.
- Try to find one thing to match each letter. For example, Tom could find the following objects:

  T—table
  O—orange
  M—mirror

Nursery Rhyme Letters

Teaches nursery rhymes

- Pick out a favorite short nursery rhyme, such as "Little Miss Muffet," "Little Jack Horner," "Hickory Dickory Dock," and "Jack and Jill."
- Show the child the nursery rhyme either in a book or on a paper where you have printed the words.
- After saying the rhyme many times, help a child find the letters in his name that are also in the nursery rhyme.
- This is a very exciting game for children because they love seeing that their name has the same letters as in a nursery rhyme.

Window Letters

Teaches creativity

- This is a nice activity to do on a dark and dreary day. It brightens up the room with painted letters on the window.
- Using either fingerpaint or tempera paint, let children paint letters on the window.
- Start with the letters in their name and then add the letters in the names of their family members.
- If the window is large enough, encourage children to paint an object and next to it, paint the letter that it begins with. For example, paint a sun and next to it, paint an "S."

Letter Detectives

Teaches letter concentration

- Fill a box or basket with lots of newspapers and magazines, highlighters, and magnifying glasses.
- Call this box "The Letter Detective."
- Give the child an assignment to look for a certain letter or group of letters. Ask him to highlight the letters.
- Ask him to find the letters in his name, find the letters or words of the day of the week, or the current month.
- Children enjoy being detectives and they particularly enjoy using a magnifying glass.

Looking at Letters Differently

Teaches creativity

- Point out to a child how many things are symmetrical. Show him how butterflies have two matching wings, and how leaves have two sides that are the same.
- Tell him that many letters have matching sides as well. Write the letters "O," "M," "U," "V," "W," and "X," and point out the matching sides.
- Another fun way to look at these letters is with a mirror. Hold the mirror over the letter both horizontally and vertically and you can see the symmetry.
- You can also look at letters based on straight lines, such as the letters "E," "F," and "T," or on curvy lines such as the letters "C," "J," and "S."
- This kind of activity helps children think with different points of view. It is highly creative.

What Does the Cook Like?

Teaches vocabulary

- You will need lots of magazine pictures of food items.
- Look at all of the pictures with a child and name the foods.
- Tell the child that the cook likes peas ("P") and ask him what other foods start with the same letter. (Have on hand pictures of pizza, pickles, peanuts, and other foods that start with the letter "P.")
- After you find several foods that start with the same letter, change the letter. Tell the child that the cook likes macaroni. Now search for "M" foods.

Letter Buffet

Teaches cognitive skills

Group Game

- This activity is fun to do with a group of children.
- Each child suggests food for a buffet. The food should start with the beginning letter of the child's name.
- Discuss what foods start with the various letter names. For example, Vicky could bring vegetables, Mary could bring marshmallows, and so on.
- Talk about the different food possibilities.
- If desired, plan a time when you can share an alphabet buffet with the group.
- The children will enjoy this very much.

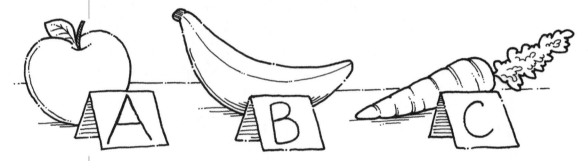

Palm Reading Game

Teaches creativity

- With a washable marker, write a letter on a child's palm.
- Say, "I am going to read your palm."
- Look at his palm and describe the letter. For example, "Your palm has a very interesting letter on it. It is a long line with a short line across it. It is called a T.
- Continue saying other words that start with the letter "T."
- Ask him to say words that start with the letter "T."
- The more descriptive you make this, the more fun it becomes.
- Encourage him to play this game with friends and family members.

Looking for Letters

Teaches cognitive skills

Group Game

- This game increases phonemic awareness and helps children identify beginning consonant sounds.
- Put small objects, such as markers, paper, small toys, coins, small blocks, crayons, small paintbrushes, and so on, in a box.
- Sit in a circle. Place the box of objects outside the circle.
- Sing the following to the tune of "The Farmer in the Dell":

  We're looking for an "A" (or another letter),
  We're looking for an "A" (or another letter),
  A/A/A/A/A/ (Sing sound of the letter to the tune of "Hi-ho, the derry-o!")
  We're looking for an "A" (or another letter).

- Ask a child to find an object in the box beginning with that sound and place it in the center of the circle.
- Continue until all objects have been used.

Uppercase Picture Cards

Teaches reading motivation

- Knowing the alphabet is a key to successful reading. There are many ways to learn the alphabet and have fun in the process.
- For this game, you will need magazines, large index cards, a box to hold the cards, scissors, glue, and a marker.
- Ask a child to help you cut out magazine pictures of objects with names that start with the letters of the alphabet, for example, a car = "C." (Each time you do this game, focus on words of 3-5 letters.)
- Glue each picture on a large index card, and at the top of the card write the letter that the picture starts with. Write the letter in uppercase.
- Keep the index cards of letters in a card box for the child to look through.

Lowercase Picture Cards

Teaches phonemic pronunciation

- This game is played the same way as the uppercase picture card game (see page 44), except that you print the lowercase letter on an index card.
- Then sort the cards and put the upper- and lowercase pictures together.
- Once the child understands this game, reverse it. Show him a letter and ask him to find a picture that starts with that letter.
- Both this game and "Uppercase Picture Cards" help children internalize necessary information for future reading.

Note: When you are teaching a letter sound, be careful not to add an "uh" sound at the end of the letter. For example, letter "S" should sound like a snake hissing, with no throat sound. Letter /s/ sounds like "sss," not "suh." If a child learns the sounds /c/, /a/, and /t/ as sounding like "kuh," "aah," and "tuh," those sounds will not come together to say "cat!"

Matching Letters

Teaches observation skills

- Add to the Alphabet Index Game (page 23) by first repeating the game. Write a letter on an index card, name the letter, and name a word that begins with that letter.
- Now mix up the index cards (both uppercase and lowercase) and help the child separate them into pairs of upper- and lowercase letters.
- This game enhances letter recognition skills.

Alphabet Chanting

Teaches different ways to sing a song

- It's great fun to sing the "Alphabet Song," and most children know it.
- Try chanting the words in different voices. Say it fast, slow, loud, soft, laughing, crying, whining, or in any other voice, focusing on the sound of the letters.
- The important thing is that children learn the letters so that they can begin to understand what sounds the letters make.
- Try singing the "Alphabet Song" any of the following ways:
  - two times slowly and two times very fast
  - in a teeny tiny voice
  - in a big, roaring voice

Sunshine Letters

Teaches fine motor skills

- You will need a sunny day for this activity.
- Take a sheet of dark construction paper (blue or black) and let the children make a letter on the paper with heavy string.
- Place the paper in a sunny indoor spot. Let it stay there for several hours.
- When you take off the string, you will have a sun print letter.

Saved by the Bell

Teaches listening skills

Group Game

- You will need a bell to ring.
- Sit with a group of children in a circle and tell them that you are going to pass around a card with a letter on it.
- When you ring the bell, whoever has the card says the name of the letter he is holding.
- As you play the game, change the way you ring the bell. Shake it slowly, fast, in patterns, and softly.
- This is a very good game to develop letter recognition.

Musical Letters

Teaches socialization

Group Game

- Give each child a card with a letter of the alphabet on it.
- Tell the children that you are going to play some music and you would like them to move around the room to the music.
- When the music stops, whoever they are standing next to will be their partner.
- Play the music and then stop the music.
- The partners look at their letters and make up a sentence using one or more words starting with the letters they are holding.
- Give each group a chance to tell their sentence, and then start the game again.

Creamy Letters

Teaches creative expression

- Cover a tabletop with shaving cream.
- Let a child make letters in the cream with his finger. Start with the letters in his name.
- If you have a digital camera, take a picture of the shaving cream name and print it out from your computer.
- Hang the picture somewhere special.

Sandpaper Letter Game

Teaches sensory skills

Group Game

- Cut out all of the alphabet letters from sandpaper.
- Encourage children to feel the letters and show them how to move their fingers up, down, and around to feel the shape.
- Pick two letters and let a child look at them, feel them, and say their names.
- Blindfold a child and give him one of the two letters and see if he can identify it by the feel.
- Or, create a set of letters with a different texture to play this game. You will need paper (cardboard is good), glue, and salt. Write a large letter on the paper. Trace with glue. Sprinkle with salt. When it is dry, use as above.

Teaches cognitive skills

- A good game to adapt for letter play is Scrabble®.
- Children love lining up the letters in the little trays.
- Let a child take out one letter at a time and put it in the tray.
- Ask him to name the letter and help him try to name different words that begin with that letter sound.
- Another game to play with him is to tell him where to put his letter. Start in the middle of the board, like any Scrabble game. Keep adding letters to make a word.

Note: This helps children look at words horizontally and vertically.

- Let him say the letters, say the sound, and say the word. For example, "cat." He would say the letter, "C," then say the sound, /c/, and then say the word, "cat."

3

Letter Sound Games

Letter sounds are the essential building blocks of speech. Knowing these sounds, technically called "phonological awareness," gives one the ability to discern the sounds in words. Word play is key to phonological awareness because it entails listening to the way words sound and recognizing how they change. Developing a sense of syllables is another key part of phonological awareness and is an important precursor to sounding out words.

Before children learn to read print, they need to understand that words are made up of speech sounds, technically called phonemes. This understanding is called phonemic awareness. The 44 phonemes in the English language are the smallest parts of sound in a spoken word that make a difference in the word's meaning. For example, changing the first phoneme in the word "hat" from /h/ to /p/ changes the word from "hat" to "pat," and so changes the meaning. Reading expert Louisa C. Moats, co-author of *Straight Talk About Reading*, says phonemic awareness is essential because our writing system is a representation of speech sounds. "Ninety percent of the time, kids who have reading problems have a weakness in their ability to detect and identify speech sounds," Moats says.

Reading milestones:

- Naming several words that begin with the same sound—bat, boy, and bell
- Replacing one sound with another—replace the first sound in pig with /d/ to make dig.

The Puppet Game

Teaches thinking skills

- Tell a child that a hand puppet is going to tell her what it likes.
- When she hears what the puppet likes, she can try to say another word that starts with the same sound.
- If the puppet says, "I like popcorn," then she needs to think of a word that starts with the /p/ sound.
- Continue playing the game, asking the child to name more than one thing that begins with the sound of the puppet's word, or the puppet can name another thing that it likes.
- Use pictures in magazines to help the child find more words.

The B Balloon

Teaches coordination

- Find pictures in magazines of items that begin with the letter "B."
- Cut out the pictures that you find. You can also cut out pictures of the letter B itself.
- Give each child a balloon and discuss that the word "balloon" also starts with the letter "B."

Caution: Balloons can be dangerous. Be certain children do not put whole balloons or pieces of balloons in their mouth.

- Blow up the balloons and glue the "B" pictures on the balloons.
- Take turns naming the pictures on the balloons. Always say the word "balloon" first and then the name of the picture. For example, balloon-bird, balloon-ball, balloon-baby.
- Have fun hitting the balloon and trying to keep it up in the air. As you are hitting it, sing the alphabet song and try to sing to the end while keeping the balloon up in the air.

Sounds to Say

Teaches cognitive skills

- You will need an alphabet chart for this game.
- Point to a letter on the chart and ask a child to say the sound.
- Continue with several letters. At first, use letters that she knows and feels comfortable saying aloud.
- Add a new letter that is a little harder. The sounds /b/ and /d/ are usually confusing, so these are good sounds to use in this game.
- When the child gets confident in this game, reverse the procedure. Say a sound and ask her to point to the letter that makes that sound.

Singing Same Sounds

Teaches listening skills

- Choose a song that you know and substitute a consonant sound for the beginning of each word in the song.
- A good way to start is by using the words from "I've Been Working on the Railroad": changing "Fee fi fiddilee i, o," to "Hee hi hiddilee hi ho," "Mee my middilee mi mo," and so on.
- Try "Old MacDonald." For cow, change the "moo, moo here…" to a /c/ sound and it becomes "coo, coo cere and a coo, coo cere." For horse, "neigh, neigh here" becomes "hey, hey here."

The First Sound Song

Teaches sight words

- On separate pieces of paper, write the names of everyone in a child's family, and names of pets, friends, and anyone the child knows.
- Put the papers in a box.
- Ask the child to pick one of the papers.
- Look at the name on the paper and sing the following song to the tune of "Mary Had a Little Lamb."

What's the first sound in this name, in this name, in this name?
What's the first sound in this name?
The first sound is _____.

- After you say the sound, see if the child can recognize the name.
- This is a game that you can play over and over again.

Singing the Vowels

Teaches order of vowels

● Sing the following song to the tune of "Bingo":

I can sing the vowels today,
I know them all by name, oh!
"A," "E," "I," "O," "U,"
"A," "E," "I," "O," "U,"
"A," "E," "I," "O," "U,"
I know them all by name!

I can sing the vowels today,
I know them all by name, oh!
[clap] *"E," "I," "O," "U,"*
[clap] *"E," "I," "O," "U,"*
[clap] *"E," "I," "O," "U,"*
I know them all by name!

I can sing the vowels today
I know them all by name, oh!
[clap, clap] *"I," "O," "U,"*
[clap, clap] *"I," "O," "U,"*
[clap, clap] *"I," "O," "U,"*
I know them all by name!

(Continue pattern.)

I can sing the vowels today,
I know their short sounds too, oh.
/a/ /e/ /i/ /o/ /u/, (sing short vowel sound for each letter)
/a/ /e/ /i/ /o/ /u/,
/a/ /e/ /i/ /o/ /u/,
I know their short sounds too!

Long Vowels Chant

Teaches rhyming

Group Game

- Divide the group into two parts.
- The first half says the first line. The second half says the second line. You say the words for "Third." Everyone says the words for "All."

First: rain, gain, train.
Second: Say, hay, may.
Third: What sound do you hear?
All: Long /a/, long /a/, long /a/.

First: Feet, heat, seat.
Second: Bee, see, tree.
Third: What sound do you hear?
All: Long /e/, long /e/, long /e/.

First: Five, dive, hive.
Second: Pie, my, hi.
Third: What sound do you hear?
All: Long /i/, long /i/, long /i/.

First: Boat, coat, goat.
Second: Hoe, go, toe.
Third: What sound do you hear?
All: Long /o/, long /o/, long /o/.

First: Tune, June, dune.
Second: Blue, glue, clue.
Third: What sound do you hear?
All: Long /u/, long /u/, long /u/.

How Many P's?

Teaches nursery rhymes

- Ask the children to say any poem that has many words that start with the letter "P." One example is:

  Peas porridge hot,
  Peas porridge cold,
  Peas porridge in the pot
  Nine days old.

- Say it a second time and accent all the words that start with the sound of the letter "P."
- Now ask children to listen as you say the poem and count how many words start with the letter "P" sound.
- Say it again and hold up a finger each time you say a word that begins with the letter "P" sound.

Matching Sounds

Teaches comparisons

- When children first learn to read and write, they need practice matching beginning sounds.
- You will need old magazines, scissors, and index cards.
- Cut out pictures from the magazines and mount them on the index cards. Select pictures that are familiar to the children, including several pictures that begin with the same sound, such as ball, boy, butter, Band-Aid, and so on.
- Turn all of the cards face down in rows.
- Ask a child to choose two cards and to turn them face up. If the objects on the cards start with the same letter sound, she keeps the match. If the beginning sounds are different, she turns the cards face down and tries again.

Sounds Around

Teaches auditory discrimination

- The sounds of words are very important to reading. One way to help children learn the sounds of words is to introduce them to real sounds in the world around them.
  - Show children a picture book with animals. Point to a picture of a dog and say, "The dog says, 'Woof, woof, woof.'" Find a picture of a cow. Say, "The cow says, 'Moo, moo, moo.'" Repeat this with pictures of other animals or birds.
  - Write a letter on a piece of paper and tell the sound that the letter makes. If you were saying "moo" for the cow, then write an M on the paper and say the /m/ sound, "Mmmmmm."
  - Use the letters that you were using with the animal sounds.

Snake Art

Teaches creativity

- You will need round white stickers, black construction paper, and white labels (to identify the child's name).
- Give children a piece of black construction paper and round white stickers.
- Encourage children to create a snake with their stickers. Snakes can be in an "S" shape and go in any direction.
- Let them identify the head of the snake by putting two black eyes on the sticker. You can do that for them when they show you where the head is.
- Ask them to put their index finger on the head and follow the shape they have made while saying the sound that the letter "S" makes.
- When they come to the end, say the word "snake."
- Put a label at the bottom of their picture and write their name on it.
- Then move in an "S" by slithering like a snake, or sound like an "S" by making hissing sounds.

What's My Sound?

Teaches cognitive thinking

Group Game

- Gather an assortment of magazine pictures that are clearly defined. For example, a police officer, (letter "P"), a firefighter (letter "F"), or a dog (letter "D").
- Show a picture to the group and ask whose name begins with the same sound as the first letter of the person, place, or thing in the picture.
- Let these children come forward and say the name of the picture and then say their name. For example, "My name is Dana and the picture is a dog."
- This is a good game because it involves cognitive thinking and gives each child a special moment.

Favorite Treats

Teaches vocabulary

- This is a fun way to practice beginning sounds.
- Ask a child to name her favorite hobby or favorite treat. Explain that whatever she names must begin with the same sound as her name.
- Help her think of words. If her name is Carla, some of the words could be "candy," "carrots," or "catch."
- Help her write her name on a piece of paper and next to her name, draw a picture of the favorites that she has chosen.

Beginning Sound Game

Teaches observation skills

- Give a child a piece of paper on which is written, "My name is _____" at the top.
- Ask the child to write her name in the blank.
- Tell the child to glue or draw pictures of items with the same beginning sound as her name.
- Repeat using the names of family members and pets.

Silly Names

Teaches that learning and humor go together

- Ask a child to say her name.
- Tell her that today you are going to call her a different name.
- Let her pick a letter and substitute that letter at the beginning of her name. If her name is Ashley and she has chosen the letter sound /p/, call her Pashley.
- Play the same game with your name and substitute the first letter. Children will love it!

The Sound Shopping Trip

Teaches cognitive skills

- You will need magazines or catalogs with pictures of objects that children recognize. Toy catalogs are very effective.
- Tell a child that she is going on a pretend shopping trip. Ask her to point to a picture of something on the page that she would like to buy on this pretend trip.
- When she points to the picture, let her tell you the name of the object. Then ask what sound the object starts with. For example, if she points to a ball, she can say the /b/ sound. Help her if needed.

It's in the Bag

Teaches size discrimination

- Pick five favorite letters. Letters in a child's name are usually their favorites.
- Take five plastic bags labeled with an upper- and lowercase version of each letter, using one bag per letter.
- Help the child search for items that begin with the sound that the letter marked on the sack makes.
- Try to find one or two items for each letter and put them in the bag.
- Share them with other family members.

I'm Thinking of a Sound

Teaches an awareness of words

- Playing with the sounds of words helps children listen to sounds and words, and develop an understanding of the language.
- Talk about different sounds of words. Start with body parts such as mouth, lips, elbow, ankle, and others.
- Point to your mouth and say, "mmmmmmouth." Ask the child to copy you.
- Look around the room and ask the child if she can think or see other words that start with the /m/ sound, such as "mirror," "muffin," "marker," and so on.
- Repeat this game using different letter sounds.

Matching Sounds

Teaches about same and different

- In order to read, children must know the sounds of letters.
- Take 10 index cards and write a capital letter on each card.
- Take another set of 10 cards and write the same letters on each one.
- Mix up the cards and lay them face down on a table.
- Ask a child to turn over one card and say the sound of the letter. For example, /t/.
- Now ask the child to turn over another card and say its sound. If the sounds are the same, the child can keep the cards. If the sounds are different, she turns the cards back over. The goal is to collect all of the cards.

Sticker Sound Story

Teaches creative storytelling

- You will need lots of stickers with pictures for this game plus two sheets of 8 ½ x 11 sheets of paper.
- Sit with a child and tell her that you are going to write a letter on a piece of paper.
- Write the letter and ask her to tell you the sound of the letter that you have written.
- When she tells you the sound, ask her to name two more words that begin with the same sound.
- When she can do that, let her choose a sticker to put on her piece of paper.
- After she has many stickers, help her make up a story about the stickers on her paper.

Same or Different

Teaches listening skills

- Review several sounds: /m/, /s/, /p/, /r/, /f/, and /l/ are good ones to start with because they are easily distinguishable from one another.
- Tell a child that you are going to say two sounds. If the sounds are the same, she should put her hands in the air. If the sounds are different, she should keep her hands to her side.
- Start with the same sounds. Make the /m/ sound two times. Make the /p/ sound two times. Remind her to put her hands in the air if the sounds are the same.
- Now, make two different sounds like /p/ and /m/.
- This game takes great listening skills and helps young children understand the sounds of letters.
- When children learn how to differentiate between two very different letter sounds, try two similar ones, such as /b/ and /d/.

Do You Hear the "S"?

Teaches alliteration

Group Game

- Play a listening game. While you tell a story, children listen for words that begin with the /s/ sound as in "silly."
- Explain that when you say a word that begins with the /s/ sound, they can clap their hands.
- Each time you say an /s/ sound word and they clap correctly, write the word on a piece of paper.
- If children clap on a word that doesn't start with /s/, ask them to listen again as you say the word with more emphasis on the beginning sound.
- When you have four or five /s/ words written down, read the words one after the other. This will be fun to say.

Sound Sentences

Teaches listening skills

- Practice saying a sentence with all of the words starting with the same sound.
- First say the sentence correctly, and then try using the same sound to begin each word.
- Use short, easy sentences to begin. For example, "The dog barked," using the letter "T," becomes, "Te tog tarked."
- This is fun but not easy and takes a lot of cognitive skill for the child.
- It is wonderful for learning sounds of letters.
- Another example for the letter "T": "Let's go outside." becomes "Tet's toe toutside."
- This can get pretty silly, which the children really enjoy.

1-2-3, Say the Sound

Teaches an understanding of ordinal position— first, second, third, and so on

- Each sound in a word is important, and it is important for children to begin to say the sounds of a word to develop their reading skills.
- Cut out pictures of familiar objects from magazines. The objects should have three sounds, such as /m/ /a/ /n/, /p/ /i/ /g/, /c/ /o/ /w/, /h/ /o/ /g/, /t/ /o/ /y/, or /p/ /e/ /n/.
- Ask a child to choose a picture. Tell her that as you hold up your fingers, she should name the sound.
- For example, if the picture is a cat, when you hold up one finger, she says /c/, two fingers, /a/, and three fingers, /t/.
- After you have done this a few times let her hold up fingers so you can say the sounds. This is a great way for her to practice it again.
- When three sounds becomes easy, move on to words with four sounds.

Listening for Sounds

Teaches cognitive skills

- This song will help children identify the beginning, middle, and ending sounds in words. For example, "What is the beginning sound in 'nice?'" or "What is the ending sound in 'run?'" or "What is the sound you hear in the middle of 'pig?'"
- You may use the same sound for each position (beginning, middle, and end) as you begin to work with a new sound and then mix them up as children learn more sounds.
- Sing the following song to the tune of "Old MacDonald Had a Farm."

What's the sound that starts these words: "butter," "ball," and "boy?"
(Wait for a response from the children—/b/.)
/b/ is the sound that starts these words: "butter," "ball," and "boy."
With a /b/, /b/, here and a /b/, /b/, there,
Here a /b/, there a /b/, everywhere a /b/, /b/.
/b/ is the sound that starts these words: "butter," "ball," and "boy."

What's the sound in the middle of these words: "peel," and "feet," and "bead?"
(Wait for a response from the children—/ee/.)
/ee/ is the sound in the middle of these words: "peel," and "feet," and "bead."
With an /ee/, /ee/, here and an /ee/, /ee/, there,
Here an /ee/, there an /ee/, everywhere an /ee/, /ee/.
/ee/ is the sound in the middle of these words: "peel," and "feet," and "bead."

What's the sound at the end of these words: "head," and "mad," and "red?"
(Wait for a response from the children—/d/.)
/d/ is the sound at the end of these words: "head," and "mad," and "red."
With a /d/, /d/, here and a /d/, /d/, there,
Here a /d/, there a /d/, everywhere a /d/, /d/.
/d/ is the sound at the end of these words: "head," and "mad," and "red."

Separating Sounds

Teaches auditory discrimination

Group Game

- This game will help children learn to separate the sounds of words from their meanings by showing them that a word can change to a new word if the initial phoneme (sound) of a word is removed or changed.

- With the children seated in a circle, explain that sometimes when you take a sound away from a word, you end up with a totally different word.

- For example, say "b-b-b-ball," elongating the first consonant, and ask the children to repeat it. Then say "all," and ask the children to repeat it.

- Ask the children if they know which sound has been taken away, and repeat the words again.

- This is very challenging for young children. Most children can identify the "hidden word" (in this case "all"), but they may need extra practice identifying what is taken away.

- Children may also be inclined to say rhyming words rather than to focus on initial sounds. Be careful not to flip back and forth between activities involving rhyming and initial sounds.

Tap the Sounds

Teaches rhythm

- Play this game while sitting at a table.
- Say a word (begin with simple words such as "dog" or "pig") and ask a child to tap on the table the number of sounds (phonemes) in the word.
- Ask the child to tell you the number of phonemes in the word. Repeat what the child says.
- Say the word again separating each sound—/d/ /o/ /g/.
- Ask the child to copy what you said.
- Continue if the child is interested.

Listen to My Rhythm

Teaches listening skills

- Listening to patterns establishes key concepts in phonemic awareness such as the ability to listen to and duplicate sounds.
- Tell the children that you are going to play a listening game in which you will clap a pattern that they will listen to, and then on your signal, they will try to copy it.
- Start with an easy pattern: two claps, pause, two claps, pause, and so on. When selecting a pattern, adjust its difficulty based on the age and maturity of the children.
- You can also make sound patterns with your voice. Pick a word and say it in a rhythmic pattern. For example, when you say "cat, cat, cat," you can say the last "cat" louder than the others.
- Ask the children to copy you.

Punch Out the Last Sound

Teaches listening skills

- This game is good for distinguishing the last sound of a word.
- Pick a word that is familiar to the children and drag your right hand from left to right across your body as you say the word.
- On the last sound of the word, punch out your hand as you say the sound.
- Encourage children to pick a word and do the same.
- Children enjoy this game very much and it is excellent for helping children hear the last sound of a word.

Jumping the Phonemes

Teaches motor skills

Group Game

- Mark the floor or sidewalk with a series of five lines (number of lines is changeable). (See illustration below.)
- The children begin by standing in a row along the first line. Explain that they must listen to the word and decide how many sounds it has. They move forward one row for every sound.
- Call out a word like "cat" and then say "begin."
- The children jump forward the number of phonemes in the word. If the child is correct (in this case, she has jumped forward three rows), she keeps her place. If incorrect, she moves back to the first line.
- The game ends when all children have been successful (jumped the correct number of times). It is important to note that the children that have the most difficult time learning phonemes need the most practice. That is why it is important to wait until all of the children are finished.

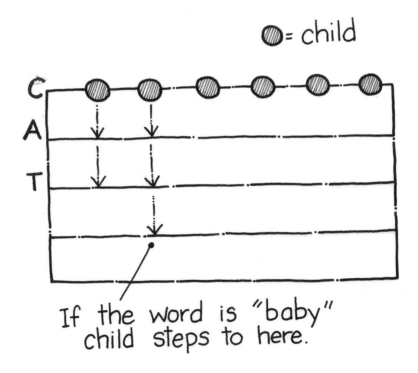

⬤ = child

If the word is "baby" child steps to here.

4

Name Games

One of the first words children learn is their own name. Children love playing games with their names and with the names of their friends, and they love hearing their names in nonsense rhymes and their favorite poems or songs whenever possible. At school, children learn to read their friends' names—on name tags, on desks, on mailboxes and cubbies, and on papers and artwork hung up for display.

Marie Clay, the author of *Becoming Literate*, says, "The use of the children's names in a class activity is a useful way of developing letter knowledge. Children will use their knowledge of letters in family names or classmates' names at later stages as part of their analysis of new words. Usually it is the initial letters that catch [the child's] attention."

A few of the concepts children can learn using names include the following:

- Directionality—left-to-right progression of print across the line
- The difference between a letter and a word
- Letter recognition and letter formation
- Phonemic awareness and sound-symbol relationships
- Consonants and vowels
- Initial, medial, and ending sounds
- Rhyming words

My Name Is _____

Teaches beginning sounds

Group Game

- Sit with the children in a circle with legs folded.
- Take a stuffed animal and pass it around as music plays.
- When the music stops, the child who is holding the stuffed animal says, "My name is _____ and it begins with the letter __."
- The child who had the turn then puts his legs out straight in front of him as a signal that he has had a turn.
- If a child who had a turn gets the stuffed animal, he gives it to the next child in the circle.

Writing Names

Teaches spelling skills

Group Game

- Young children usually learn to write their name before any other word.
- Create situations that require children to write their name.
- Here are some ideas:
  - Ask children to write their name on paper that they will use to create artwork.
  - Autograph Party: Give each child a piece of paper. Each child takes his paper and asks every other child to write his name (autograph) on his paper. You can also encourage the children to draw a picture next to their name.
  - Put photographs of children on poster board. Encourage them to write a friend's name next to their picture. The friends can offer help spelling their names.

Musical Names

Teaches listening skills

Group Game

- Write the first names of all the children on individual pieces of paper and place them in a box.
- Ask the children to sit in a circle and pass the box around as the music plays.
- When the music stops, whoever has the box gets to pick a piece of paper from the box.
- He reads the name on the paper. If he has trouble reading the name, you can help him.
- The child whose name is read stands up and takes a bow as the other children applaud him.
- If more than one child has the same name, they all stand up at the same time. Continue with the game.

Who Is Here?

Teaches about similarities and differences

Group Game

- Sit in a circle.
- You will need index cards with one child's name on each card.
- Hold up a card with a name on it.
- When a child sees his name, ask the child to say, "Good morning."

Note: This is also good for name recognition for all of the children in the group.

- You could also teach the children to say "good morning" in several languages.

Cantonese (China)—"Jo san."

Creole (Dominican Republic)—"Bon jou."

Esperanto (international use)—"Bonan matenon."

French (Europe, Africa, Canada)—"Bonjour."

German (Central Europe)—"Guten Morgen."

Greek (Greece, Cyprus)—"Kalimera."

Hebrew (Israel)—"Boker tov."

Japanese (Japan)—"Ohayo."

Russian (Russia)—"Dobroye utro."

Zulu (Southern Africa)—"Umhlala gahle."

Spanish (America, Spain)—"Buenos días."

Italian (Cent. Europe, E Africa)—"Buon giorno."

Learning and Spelling Names

Teaches observation skills

Group Game

- Sit in a circle and say the following:

  A name is very special.
  What is your name? (One child says his name.)
  A name is very special.
  Let's all say your name. (Everyone says the name.)

- Continue until each child has had a chance to say his name.
- Give each child a card with his name printed on it and the child holds it so that it is facing everyone else when it is his turn.
- Repeat the game again and spell the names of the children.

Where's Your Name?

Teaches observation skills

- Print a child's name on an index card.
- Print names of family members and pets on other index cards. Use names that he knows.
- Put all of the cards on the floor and ask the child to find the card with his name on it.
- When he finds it, say the names of the letters with him.
- Continue with another name.

Finding Names

Teaches observation skills

Group Game

- Using upper- and lowercase letters, write each child's name on a separate piece of construction paper. Make the letters large.
- Ask the children to hide their eyes as you place the name cards around the room.
- When the children open their eyes, ask them to look for their own name.
- When they have found their name, they can sit down on the floor until everyone has finished.
- Children really enjoy this game. A variation of this game is to make several copies of each child's name and tell them how many names they should look for.

New Names

Teaches an awareness of nature

- Make up new names with children using ideas from nature, such as Wendy Wind, Running Randy, or Fred Fox.
- Say the following poem:

Names **by Jackie Silberg**
Your name is very special.
Your name belongs to you.
And if you listen to your name,
It will tell you what to do.

- Children say their name and the letter and sound it begins with. Encourage them to act out their new name.
- You can also give new names to family members and pets.

The Letters in My Name

Teaches cognitive skills

Group Game

- Once a group of children have learned to recognize their own name and are able to spell their name, give them directions based on the letters in their name.
- For example:
  - If you have "P" in your name, jump up and then sit down.
  - If you have an "R" in your name, clap your hands.
  - If you have an "M" in your name, stomp your feet.
- This game takes a lot of cognitive thinking and develops listening skills.

Letters in Your Name

Teaches auditory discrimination

- Write a child's name on a piece of paper and look at it with him.
- Say the names of the letters out loud.
- Tell him that you are going to say a letter and tell him to do an action. If the letter is in his name, he must do the action. If the letter is not in his name, he must sit perfectly still.
- For example, if his name is Caleb, say, "'C'—jump up and down." Then he jumps up and down. Then say, "'X'—raise your hand." This time he sits perfectly still.
- This game is a lot of fun, and you can focus on developing children's motor skills.

Reading Names

Teaches comparison skills

- This game will help children learn the first letter of their name and learn the first letter of names of family members.
- Write a child's name and other family members' names on each index card (one name per card). Include friends and pets.
- Go through all of the cards and talk about each name and whose names they are.
- Go through the cards again and talk about the beginning letter of each person's name.
- Compare names to see if any of them start with the same letter.
- Compare ending sounds and number of syllables in the name.

David

Grandma

Uncle Joe

Bingo

Rolling for Names

Teaches motor skills

Group Game

- Make a nametag for each child.
- Sit in a circle.
- Call a child by name and roll a ball to him.
- Tell the child that when you hold up his nametag, he is to roll the ball back to you.
- Hold up two or three other names before you hold up the child's name. When you hold up his name, remind him to roll back the ball.
- Continue with another child.

Name Fishing

Teaches about magnets

Group Game

- In advance, place paper clips on children's nametags and place them in a large container.
- Sit in a circle and place the container in the center of the circle.
- The center of the circle is the "pond" and the children take turns using magnetic fishing poles to "catch a name fish."
- The child whose name is on the card says his name to let everyone know that it was his name that was caught.
- The child whose name was caught fishes for the next name.

Singing Names

Teaches letter recognition

Group Game

- Sit in a circle and sing the following to the tune of "This Old Man."

If your name
Starts with "A,"
Stand right up and take a bow.
Can you tell us, please,
Please tell us your name?

- As the last line of the song, the child says, "My name is _____."
- Continue with the next child.
- Try combining letters, for example:

If your name
Starts with "A," "B," or "C,"
Stand right up and take a bow…

The Book of Names

Teaches how books are written

- Names are very important to young children. This activity will teach children letter formation, alphabetical order, and left-to-right progression.
- Staple together sheets of paper with one letter of the alphabet on each page. The pages should be in alphabetical order.
- Put both upper- and lowercase letters in red on each page.
- Each day write a name in the book. The letter that the name begins with is the page that you will write on.
- Let a child tell you whose name he wants to write, and guide him to the correct page for that name.
- Start with family names, pet names, names of the child's favorite people, and so on. Soon you will have a book of names that the child will be able to read.

Name Game

Teaches creativity

Group Game

- Children sit in a circle and take turns saying their names.
- The first time around, they whisper their names and say the beginning sound of their name.
- The next time around they shout their name. Always follow the name with the beginning sound.
- Other ways to say your name are sing, fast, slowly, and in a gruff voice. What other ways can you think of? Ask the children for their suggestions.

Letter Tasks

Teaches sound awareness

- Children are very proud of their names. Suggest that they make a list of things that they can do that start with each letter of their names.
- For example, if the child's name is Scott, he could say:
  - S—sing a song
  - C—call a friend
  - O—open a door
  - T—tap dance
  - T—try a somersault
- They will enjoy thinking of all the things they can do with the letters of their names. This will also increase their awareness of sounds.

Cheering Names

Teaches spelling skills

Group Game

- Write a child's name on paper or a white board.
- Turn the name into a cheer.
- As you say the cheer, point to each letter in their name and have the children join you. For example, for the name "Caleb":

"C," give me a "C."
"A," give me an "A.'
"L," give me an "L."
"E," give me an "E."
"B," give me a "B."
What does that spell?
Caleb, Yaaaaay!

Find Your Name

Teaches matching skills

- Print a child's name on a piece of paper in large letters.
- Give him a newspaper or magazine page.
- Help him find the letters that are in his name.
- Cut out the letters that you find and paste them on the paper.
- Help him make his name with the cut-out letters.

Clapping Names

Teaches matching skills

- This game introduces children to an understanding of syllables by clapping and counting the syllables in their own names.
- Pronounce the first name of a child syllable by syllable while clapping it out.
- Ask the child to say and clap the name along with you, and then ask, "How many syllables did you hear?"
- Once the child has caught on, ask him to clap and count the syllables in his own name.
- Compare different names. Which name has two syllables? Which name has three syllables?
- After determining the number of syllables in a name, ask the child to hold two fingers horizontally under his chin, so he can feel his chin drop for each syllable. To maximize this effect, encourage him to elongate or stretch each syllable.

Bippity Bippity Bumblebee

Teaches listening skills

Group Game

- Chant the following:

  Bippity, bippity, bumblebee,
  Tell me what your name should be.

- Ask a child to say his name. The other children repeat his name out loud.
- Continue with one of the following:
  - "Clap it!" (Children repeat the name, enunciating and clapping to each syllable.)
  - "Whisper it!" (Children whisper each syllable while clapping the name.)
  - "Silent!" (Children repeat the name, silently enunciating syllables with mouth movement.)

Hole Punch Letters

Teaches fine motor skills

- This activity helps children practice learning the letters in their name.
- You will need a hole punch, glue stick, different colors of construction paper, and a container to hold all of the punched circles.
- Punch out as many small circles in different colors of construction paper as possible.
- Write a child's name on a large piece of construction paper. Make the letters large.
- The child traces over the letters with a glue stick.
- He then sprinkles or places the construction paper circles on the letters of his name.
- This looks very beautiful when finished and the child has had practice in learning about his name and the letters in it.

Note: A variation of this activity is to use buttons or other art materials instead of hole punches.

5

Oral Blending and Segmenting Games

There are many skills related to phonemic awareness, but research has found that blending and segmentation are the two critical skills that must be taught for successful phonemic awareness. Instruction must focus on blending and segmenting words at the phoneme, or sound, level.

Blending and segmenting help children develop an understanding of the relationship between the sounds in words, and it improves their ability to manipulate sounds.

These games help children hear how sounds are put together to make words so that they can begin sounding out words independently as they read.

Say the Sound

Teaches sound recognition

Group Game

- Make letter cards for several simple words, for example, letters "c," "a," and "t" for cat. "Cat" would have three cards.
- Make enough cards so each child has a card.
- Call out the first sound of the word (the sound /c/ for "cat"). The child holding that letter card should come to the front of the room.
- Continue calling the other sounds in the word sequentially, lining the children up from left to right.
- After the word has been made, ask each cardholder to say the sound of her letter.
- Ask the rest of the children to blend the sounds to say the word.
- Continue playing the game with a new word, allowing each child to have a turn.

What's the Word?

Teaches vocabulary

- Orally segment a word and ask a child to guess the word.
- Say that that you are thinking of an animal on a farm. Say, "/c/ /ow/." Let her tell you "cow."
- Continue with other animals. It's best to say the words in a particular classification as it makes it easier for them to associate the sounds.
- Other classifications could be household objects, numbers, colors, and shapes.

Sing the Phonemes

Teaches auditory discrimination

- The song "The Wheels on the Bus" repeats the lyrics, "'round and 'round," three times.
- Replace these lyrics with three phonemes that make a word. For example, to the tune of "The Wheels on the Bus," sing:

The sounds in the word go /h/ /a/ /t/, /h/ /a/ /t/, /h/ /a/ /t/.
The sounds in the word go /h/ /a/ /t/.
Do you know the word?

- Sing the song using other words with three sounds.

The Three-Sound Game

Teaches ordinal sequence

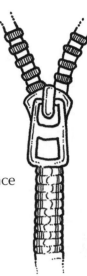

- This game helps children learn to connect sounds to make words.
- Tell a child that you are going to say three sounds. Ask her to repeat the sounds and then say the word from listening to the sounds.
- Give her an example: /d/ /o/ /g/ and then say, "dog."
- Here are some ideas for words. Remember that the word can have more than three letters. You just have to pronounce it in three parts. It's best to use words that your child can visualize. Suggestions include:

/b/ /ir/ /d/
/h/ /i/ /m/
/d/ /e/ /sk/
/c/ /ol/ /d/
/st/ /o/ /p/
/h/ /a/ /t/
/c/ /oa/ /t/
/z/ /ipp/ /er/

Baseball Blending

Teaches basic baseball rules

Group Game

- Divide the group into two teams. Select parts of the room to be first, second, third, and home base.
- You are the pitcher. The pitcher says a word in parts, such as, "/c/ /a/ /t/."
- If the child who is "at bat" can successfully blend the word, she goes to first base.
- Continue just as in baseball, with each team earning a point when a child makes it to home base.

Find the Sound

Teaches listening skills

- Draw three boxes, connected horizontally, on a sheet of paper.
- Give a child some place markers, such as bottle caps or checkers.
- Explain that you are going to say a list of words. They will all have the sound /s/ in the word. Sometimes the sound will be at the beginning, sometimes in the middle, and sometimes at the end.
- Tell the child to put her marker where she hears the /s/ sound. If it's at the beginning, she puts it in the first box. If the sound of /s/ is in the middle, the marker will go in the middle box, and the last box will indicate an /s/ at the end of the word.
- Say the following words: "silly," "happiness," "missing," "mister," "sad," and "bus."
- Try the same game with the letter "N": "running," "never," "corn," "spoon," "nickel," and "wonder."
- Integrating phonemics into everyday life helps ensure children's long-term reading success.

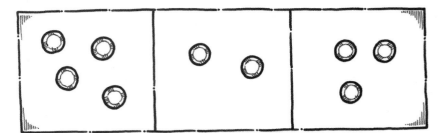

Listen for the Sound

Teaches cognitive thinking

- Identifying the beginning, middle, and ending sounds in a word takes a lot of concentration.
- To help children learn to identify the sounds, ask, "What is the ending sound in dog?" "What sound do you hear in the middle of bat?"
- When children have to listen for sounds, it takes focus and visualization.

Stretching Names

Teaches listening skills

Group Game

- This game teaches children to blend isolated sounds into a word by saying the word fast.
- Say to the children that you are going to say someone's name stretched out very slowly and then you will say it fast. For example, say, "Ssssss-aaaaaaaa-rrrrrrrr-uhhhhhh—Sarah."
- After you have done this with several names, let the children choose a name to say.
- Tell the children that you will give them a signal (such as raising your hand in the air) when it is time for all the children to say the word fast.
- Some children will need extra help with this. It is an important activity for understanding and saying sounds.
- Stretching out words draws attention to the place of each sound (beginning, middle, and end) in a word and makes spelling and decoding easier.

Which Is First?

Teaches about first, middle, and last sounds

- This game strengthens children's understanding of first, middle, and last sounds. You will need a wooden spoon for this game.
- Tap the spoon on the floor and listen to the sound.
- Tap the spoon on a table and listen to the sound.
- Tap the spoon on another spoon and listen to the sound.
- Hit the spoon on all three surfaces and say, "This sound is first (hit the spoon on the floor), this sound is in the middle (hit the spoon on the table), and this sound is last (hit the spoon on another spoon)."
- Ask the children to repeat what you have done and identify first, middle, and last sounds.

Poem Segments

Teaches nursery rhymes

- Tell the children that you are going to say a poem to them and every once in a while you will stretch out a word in the poem.
- Ask them to listen for the word that you have stretched out.
- Say the poem "Little Boy Blue." Somewhere in the rhyme, stretch out the word "boy."

Little Boy Blue, come blow your horn,
The sheep's in the meadow, the cow's in the corn.
But where is the boy who looks after the sheep?
He's under a haystack fast asleep.
Will you wake him? No, not I,
For if I do, he's sure to cry.

- When the children tell you the word that you have stretched out, say it together without stretching the word.
- Now, say the poem without stopping to segment the word.
- Continue with other nursery rhymes.

Beginning Blends

Teaches sound awareness

- To practice beginning blends, say the following tongue twisters.
- For "th" try:

Theophilus Thistle, the successful thistle sifter,
Thrust three thousand thistles through the thick of his thumb.

- For "sh" try:

She sells seashells by the seashore,
By the seashore, she sells seashells.

Sing the Sound

Teaches rhythmic awareness

- Sing the following to the tune of "Old MacDonald Had a Farm."

  Here's a sound that we can sing,
  /s/ /s/ /s/ /s/ /s/.
  You can let your voices ring,
  /s/ /s/ /s/ /s/ /s/.
  With an /s/ /s/ here and an /s/ /s/ there
  Here a /s/, there a /s/, everywhere a /s/ /s/.
  Here's a sound that we can sing,
  /s/ /s/ /s/ /s/ /s/.

- Say words that start with the sound /s/.
- Continue with another letter. It's good to use sounds that are in children's names.

Turtle Talk

Teaches listening skills

- Read or tell the story of "The Tortoise and the Hare."
- Tell the children that turtles move very slowly and talk very slowly.
- Tell them that you are going to have a "turtle talk" with them.
- Say words slowly, one at a time, articulating each sound. For example, "L-e-t'-s/r-e-a-d/a/b-o-o-k." Encourage her to respond by talking very slowly.
- This is wonderful phonemic practice.

Clapping Syllables

Teaches rhythmic expression

- Clap your hands on each syllable of a word. Ask the children to clap with you as you say the following words: "happy," "banana," "wonderful," "breakfast," and "television."
- Name other words that are familiar to the children. Say the words and let the children clap the syllables.
- Explain how hearing the parts of a word will help them learn to read better.
- Let the children suggest words to clap together, such as their favorite toy, color, or food.

Names of Toys

Teaches cognitive skills

- Place three or four favorite toys in a basket. Use a car, a doll, a ball, and any other familiar toy.
- Tell a child that you are going to pick a toy and say its name in a different way.
- Pick up the car and say the sounds "/c/ /ar/." Now say the word "car."
- Ask the child to repeat the word with you, first breaking the word into two parts and then saying the entire word.
- Continue with the rest of the toys in the basket.
- Ask the child to draw a picture of each toy that you named. Write the name of the toy on their picture and say the words again.

Reading the Snake Way

Teaches fine motor skills

- Draw a wavy line on a piece of paper.
- Draw the lowercase letter "S" at the beginning of the line. Take your pencil and draw more lowercase "S's" along the line until you come to the end of the line where you write the word "snake."
- As you are drawing the sssss, say the sound at the same time. At the end, say the word "snake."
- Pick another word like "mad" and do the same thing. Say and draw lowercase letter "M's" until the end of the line and then write "mad" as you say the word.
- Let children make other words the "snake way." Some good ones are "fan," "red," "sat," and "dim."
- Children become excited about reading when they begin to use the letter sounds that they know to read words. This is a very effective oral blending game.

6

Rhyming Games

The easiest forms of phonemic awareness for most children to acquire are those of rhyming and alliteration. Awareness of when words rhyme and how to create rhyming words is an important prerequisite to the use of rhymes or word families (word endings with the same graphophonic pattern) to decode unfamiliar words.

Even before a child learns the letters of the alphabet, he can say the sounds in his language. When he can hear the sounds in a word and tell where the sounds occur in the word, he is developing pre-reading skills. Rhyming games can help children become more aware of the sounds of language.

Focusing on the sounds of the endings of words written or spoken is the first phonological awareness skill to develop. When young children say rhymes, fingerplays, and songs, they are developing a sense of the phonological structure of language. By saying these rhyming patterns over and over, children develop the ability to recognize, identify, and then produce rhymes.

It is very important to practice rhyming first with pictures and sounds, not words in print!

One-Syllable Rhymes

Teaches sound awareness

- Choose one-syllable words that are easy to rhyme such as "had," "rat," "man," "fall," "ten," "red," "big," "fill," "hop," "dog," "bug," and "sun."
- Put these words on index cards and put the cards in a box. A shoebox works well.
- Ask a child to choose a card, for example, "ten."
- Go through the alphabet with him and think of as many words as you can. Write down the words so that he can see them: "Ben," "den," "hen," "men," "pen," "Zen."
- This gives him an opportunity to see the word and say it. He will see that the ending of each word is the same.

Rhyming Poetry

Teaches imagination

- Make up three lines of a four-line poem and encourage children to add the last line to rhyme with the second line of the poem.
- Here are some examples.

    Johnny was a boy,
    And Johnny went to bed.
    He turned off the light,
    And _____.

    I picked up a dish.
    I picked up a spoon.
    I went outside,
    And _____.

    I went to the zoo,
    And looked at a fox.
    The fox looked at me,
    And _____.

- For younger children, use two-line poems. You say the first and encourage them to add the second, such as:

    Little Mary Brown
    Went to _____.

    Scooter, Scooter, run, run, run
    Isn't this _____?

Nursery Rhyme Rhymes

Teaches about literature and nursery rhymes

- Nursery rhymes are full of wonderful words that charm children with language.
- Point out the rhyming parts of familiar nursery rhymes.
- Start by saying a line from a familiar rhyme, such as "Little Miss **Muffet** sat on her **tuffet**." As you say the rhyme, accent the rhyming words.
- Now ask the children to say the poem with you and accent the words that you accent.
- Now say the rhyme, pausing before each rhyming word and letting the children fill in the rhyming words.
- Pick a favorite and after you have said it many times, leave out the rhyming word for the child to fill in. For example:

Hickory dickory dock,
The mouse ran up the _____.

- Add rhythm instruments to this game. Each time a child says the rhyming word, he can hit a rhythm instrument at the same time.
- Some good songs or nursery rhymes for this game are "Diddle Diddle Dumpling," "Hey Diddle Diddle," "Little Boy Blue," "Old Mother Hubbard," "Old King Cole," "Little Jack Horner," "Mary Had a Little Lamb," "Eensy Weensy Spider," and "This Old Man."

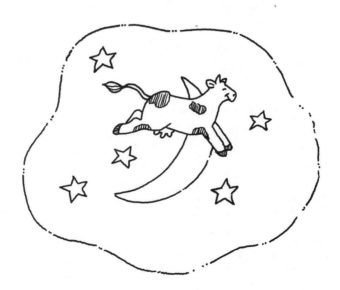

Rhyming Books

Teaches listening, language, and cognitive skills

- Select a rhyming book and read it to a child.
- Read it a second time and leave out the last word in one of the rhyming sentences.
- Let the child fill in the missing word.
- Try to make up other words that rhyme in this sentence. It's okay if the words do not make sense. It's hearing the rhyme that is important.
- The following books of rhymes are a few suggestions:
  - *Arroz Con Leche: Popular Songs and Rhymes from Latin America* by Lulu Delacre
  - *Cockadoodle Moo* compiled by John Foster
  - *The Hairy Hamster Hunt and Other Poems About Your Pets* compiled by Tony Bradman
  - *Old Mother Hubbard and Her Wonderful Dog* by James Marshall
  - *Poems for the Very Young* selected by Michael Rosen
  - *The Oxford Nursery Rhyme Book* by Iona Opie and Peter Opie
  - *The Real Mother Goose* illustrated by Blanche Fisher Wright

The Disappearing House

Teaches fine motor skills

- Draw a picture of a house on a chalkboard. Draw a door, two windows, and a chimney; a yard with fence, two flowers, grass, and a tree. Draw a sun in the sky.
- Say the following rhymes and leave out a rhyming word.
- When the child says the rhyming word, she erases that word from the picture.

Day is done, erase the___. (sun) (Erase the sun.)

Count to three, erase the ____. (tree) (Erase the tree.)

- Continue this way with every rhyming word.

I count to four, erase the _____. (door)

*Find your key and erase the chim___. (chim**ney**)*

*If you can do so, erase the win___. (win**dow**)*

Here comes showers, erase the _____. (flowers)

There's a mouse! Erase the _____! (house)

- Try playing the same game using pictures from magazines, cutting out the rhyming words.

Substituting Sounds

Teaches listening skills

- This is a challenging and fun game to play.
- Ask a child, "What rhymes with dog and starts with the sound /h/?"(hog)
  "What rhymes with can and starts with the sound /f/?" (fan)
- When the child is doing well with this game, make it a little harder.
  "What rhymes with log and starts with the sound /fr/?" (frog)
- Continue blending two consonants for the rhyming word.

The Rhyming Clown Face

Teaches fine motor skills

- Draw a clown with a child as you say the following rhyme.
- Let the child fill in the rhyming word before you draw the next step.

When drawing a clown, it is said
To always start with his_____. (head)
   (Draw a circle for a head.)
On his body, what will he wear?
On his head, he has red curly _____. (hair)
   (Add the red curly hair.)
When people laugh, he wants to hear,
So on each side, give him a great big ____. (ear) (Draw an ear on each
   side of the face.)
Now make him look very wise
By giving him two big _____. (eyes) (Draw two eyes.)
And now as everybody knows
Give him a great big _____. (nose) (Draw a nose.)
Now make a line as long as a mile
And give our clown a great big _____. (smile) (Draw a smile.)
Now our clown face is all done!
      Author unknown

Clap the Rhyme

Teaches rhythmic patterns

- Read a book of rhymes with a child. Some excellent books are listed on page xxx.
- Read the book several times so that the child can hear the patterns and rhythms of the poem.
- Pick out two or three favorites and say them together many times.
- Say a rhyme and leave out the rhyming word. Ask the child to fill in the word.

Jack and Jill
Went up the _____.

- Say it again and in addition to saying the rhyming word, clap your hands at the same time.
- Play this clapping game with many rhymes.

Claps

Teaches coordination

- Start with a simple clapping pattern: clap, say a word; clap, say a word that rhymes with the first word. For example, clap, "cat"; clap, "hat"; clap, "sat"; clap "rat."
- Try clapping two times and then saying a word.
- Try another pattern: clap, clap, snap, (word); clap, clap, snap, (rhyming word); and so on.
- Another variation is I Say and You Say. For example:
  - "I say 'dog,' and you say 'hog.'"
  - "I say 'pig,' and you say '_____.'"
  - "I say 'red,' and you say '_____.'"

Same or Different

Teaches listening skills

- Play a rhyming game where children listen to the words and tell you if the ending sounds in the words are the same or different.
- Say "cat" and "hat" and ask if they sound the same or different.
- Try other word combinations, such as "jog" and "dog," or "   " and "monkey." Again, ask if the ending sound is the same or different.
- Make up rhymes for the children's names, such as "Jack-crack" and "Mary-berry."
- Now take a child's name and pair it with a word that has a completely different sound, such as "Mary" and "asparagus," "Jack" and "ball," and so on.
- Ask if the ending sounds in the words are the same or different.

Sit Down Rhymes

Teaches motor skills

Group Game

- The children walk around in a big circle taking one step each time you say a rhyming word.
- When you say a word that doesn't rhyme, the children sit down.
- For example, say, "cat, bat, fat, door." The children sit down when they hear "door." Or say, "key, bee, flea, elephant." The children sit down when they hear "elephant."

Thumbs Up for Rhymes

Teaches observation skills

- Say two words. If the words rhyme, the children hold up their thumbs. If they do not rhyme, they keep their hands to their sides.
- Say, "cat" and "sat." They hold up their thumbs.
- Say, "tree" and "car." They keep their hands to their sides.
- Continue with sets of rhyming words and set of words that do not rhyme.
- This is a great game to play when you are waiting or when you have a few spare moments.

Roger Dodger

Teaches motor skills

- Say the following chant while jumping on each syllable.

  Roger, dodger, bodger, codger, sodger, nodger, 1, 2, 3.
  Roger, dodger, bodger, codger, sodger, nodger, 1, 2, stop. (Stop jumping.)

- Pick another name and play the same game.
- Rhyme the name with the letters of your choice.

Sticker Rhymes

Teaches drawing skills

- Take a piece of 8 ½ x11 sheet of paper and fold it into fourths.
- In each section, place a sticker of an item that can be rhymed easily with another word.
- The child draws a picture of a word that rhymes with the picture on the sticker.
- Ask the child to say the name of the sticker and then the name of his drawing.
- Print both names under the sticker so that he can see similarities in the words.

Match the Rhyme

Teaches writing skills

- Cut out four or five pictures of animals or objects and paste them on a piece of paper, for example, a cat, dog, block, or spoon.
- On the same paper, print words that rhyme with the pictures, such as "hat," "log," "clock," and "moon."
- Help children find the word that rhymes with the picture.
- Once you have played this game a few times, let children find other pictures to cut out. Help them say words that rhyme and when you find a good word, print it under the picture.

Finding Rhymes

Teaches rhyming sounds, writing skills, and recognizing words and word families

- You will need a magazine or catalog, scissors, glue stick, stapler, drawing paper, crayons, and a die.
- Staple together three or four sheets of paper. Ask the child to make a cover for the book.
- Give the child a magazine or catalog. Ask him to cut out a picture for each page of the book and glue it on the paper.
- Help him write the name of the picture under it.
- Roll the die to determine how many rhyming words will be written under each picture.
- If the picture is a dog and the die landed on the number five, then you will write five words that rhyme with dog. The words can be real or silly, such as "hog," "log," "fog," "jog," and "pog."
- Continue until all of the pages have been filled. You can always add more pages.

A Rhyme Picture

Teaches expressive art

- Tell one child that you will use rhyming words to draw a picture together.
- Sit with him at a table with crayons and paper for you and for him.
- Say two words that rhyme—"head" and "bed."
- Now say the first word only and let him say the rhyming word.
- With him, draw a picture of the rhyming word that he just said.
- Repeat with two different rhyming words.
- Again, draw a picture of the rhyming words that he has said. Remember to draw only the pictures of the rhyming word that the child has said.
- Soon you will have a rhyme picture. You can point to one of the drawings and ask the child to say the rhyming word to go with it.

A Rhyme Book for You

Teaches rhyme awareness

- Make blank books by stapling together five blank pages.
- Clip a different picture at the top of each page.
- The children draw pictures of objects that rhyme with the picture on the page, or they cut out rhyming pictures found in magazines.
- Ask the children to read their rhyme books to you.

Finish the Rhyme

Teaches listening skills

- Start this game by saying one word and asking a child to say a word that rhymes. Remember that the rhyming word can be a nonsense word.
- When you have done this a few times, say three words. The first two words should rhyme, but the third should not. The child rhymes the third word, for example, "Mary, dairy, fat, _____."
- This is hard to do because the child has to listen very carefully.

Down by the Bay

Teaches imagination

- This song is wonderful for practicing and making up rhymes.
- After you have sung it, let children illustrate their favorite verse.

Down by the Bay

*Down by the bay, where the water-
melons grow,
Back to my home, I dare not go.
For if I do, my mother will say:
"Did you ever see a goose kissing a moose
Down by the bay?"*

*Refrain:
"Did you ever see a whale with a
polka-dotted tail
Down by the bay?"*

*Refrain:
"Did you ever see a fly, wearing a tie
Down by the bay?"*

*Refrain:
"Did you ever see a bear combing his hair
Down by the bay?"*

*Refrain:
"Did you ever see llamas, eating their pajamas
Down by the bay?"*

*Refrain:
"Did you ever see a time when you couldn't make a rhyme
Down by the bay?"*

Food Rhymes

Teaches vocabulary

- Ask a child to say the rhyming word in the following sentences.
  - *Eat some corn and blow a _____.* (horn)
  - *Eat some pickles and spend some _____.* (nickels)
  - *Eat some peas and eat some _____.* (cheese)
  - *Eat some steak and bake a _____.* (cake)
  - *Eat a pear and comb your _____.* (hair)
  - *Eat a tomato and fry a _____.* (potato)
  - *Eat some fish and make a _____.* (wish)
  - *Eat a plum and wiggle your _____.* (thumb)
  - Draw a picture using all of the foods in the rhymes.
  - Make up your own rhymes with different themes. Animals and parts of the body are fun for making up rhymes.

Rhymes Around the Room

Teaches thinking skills

- Point to objects around the room and say their names.
- For example, point to a hat, and then ask a child to say as many words as he can that rhyme with "hat."
- Other easily rhymed words are "ball," "rug," "sink," "clock," "boat," and "chair."
- Remember, it's okay to use some nonsense words mixed in with actual words, such as "bat," "fat," "gat," "vat," and "cat."

Body Name Rhyme

Teaches cognitive skills

- Explain that rhyming words have the same sound at the end of the word.
- Point to something on your body, and then say a word. For example, point to your knee, and then say the word "bee."
- Ask the children what you are pointing to. Say, "The rhyming word is 'knee.'" The visual cue tells them the word and at the same time, they hear the rhyme.
- At the beginning, this may be hard, but the more you play the game, the better they will be able to hear the rhyme.
- Additional ideas include:

  - deer-ear
  - pail-nail
  - sack-back
  - go-toe
  - gum-thumb
  - put-foot
  - bye-eye
  - deck-neck

  - see-knee
  - bear-hair
  - fin-chin
  - band-hand
  - peek-cheek
  - farm-arm
  - feel-heel

- Once children feel comfortable with this game, try doing the opposite. Point to your knee and ask the children to say a rhyming word.

Silly Sentence Game

Teaches listening and language skills

- When children think of words that rhyme and put them into a sentence, they are practicing a combination of listening and language skills.
- Choose two rhyming words and ask a child to make a sentence with them.
- For example, "cat" and "hat." The child could say, "My cat is wearing a big hat."
- An easy way to start this game is to try to rhyme the names of colors. "Shoe" and "blue" could turn into "I took a shoe and painted it blue."

Partner Rhymes

Teaches listening and social skills

Group Game

- One child says, "I say 'bump,' and you say, '_____.'"
- The second child says a rhyming word such as "jump," "lump," or "dump."
- Play this game using different voices. For example, a child says in a whisper voice, "I say 'house,' and you say '_____.'"
- The second person rhymes the word and copies the kind of voice.
- Examples of different voices include loud, whisper, soft, whiny, high, and low.
- Children love to play this game.

Rhyming Fun

Teaches listening skills

Group Game

- This game needs three or four people.
- The first child says a word, for example "happy."
- The next child rhymes the word, for example "nappy."
- The third child rhymes again, for example "pappy."
- The last child says a word that doesn't rhyme, for example "pajamas."
- Everyone says all of the words together in the same order—happy, nappy, pappy, pajamas.

Note: Remember that it's the rhyme that's important. The word does not need to be an actual word.

- This game is a lot of fun and usually a lot of laughs, too!

Rhyming Names

Teaches fun with language

- Say a child's name and think up several words that rhyme with his name. The words can be nonsense words. For example, for Carlos, the rhyming words could be "barlos," "sarlos," "darlos," "marlos," and so on.
- Throughout the day when talking to him, use a word that rhymes with his name instead of his actual name. "Barlos, time for lunch." "Do you want to go outside, Darlos?"
- Once you have played this game a few times, try this with other names that he knows, such as the names of his pets, relatives, and friends.
- Practice lots of rhymes with each name before you try another name.

Me-O My-O

Teaches fun with names

Group Game

- Stand in a circle. First child walks around the circle and sings the following to the tune of "Skip to My Lou."

  Me-O My-O who should I choose? (Repeat three times.)
  I choose _____. (Name a child and rhyme his name—Mickey-Wickey.)

- Now it is Mickey's turn to walk around the circle and choose the next child whose name he will rhyme.
- This game is great fun, and the children love to rhyme the names, such as "Sarah-barah," "Betty-wetty," "Bob-mob," and so on.
- Rhyme your name too!

7 Sequencing Games

Sequencing is a very important pre-reading skill. Whether it is a story sequence, a word sequence (often found in songs), or a sound sequence of letters, beginning readers need sequencing experiences to make sense of the words and the sounds of reading.

Sequencing activities develop phonemic awareness by helping children learn to hear and identify sounds. These games will also help develop fluency, vocabulary, and comprehension skills.

Aunt Sally

Teaches vocabulary

Group Game

- This is an old and very popular childhood game, and it is wonderful for helping children learn sequencing.
- The first person says, "I'm going to visit Aunt Sally and I am taking some chocolate."
- The next person says, "I'm going to visit Aunt Sally and I am taking some chocolate and a basketball."
- Keep taking turns and the sentence gets longer and longer.
- Play this game focusing on themes, such as food, transportation, and animals.
- Another idea is to say words that all begin with the same sound.

Sequencing Songs

Teaches memory skills

- Some sequencing songs are "The Old Lady Who Swallowed a Fly," "Bingo," "Farmer in the Dell," "I Had a Rooster," and "What Do You Like?" by Jackie Silberg.

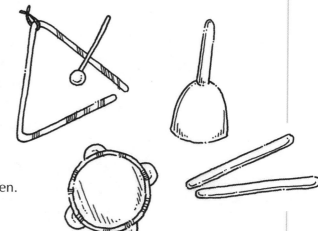

- Sometimes sequencing songs are called "add-on" songs.
- Sing these songs with the children.

Sing in Order

Teaches coordination

- A wonderful sequencing song that children enjoy is "Head, Shoulders, Knees, and Toes."
- Touch the parts of the body as you sing the song.

Head, shoulders, knees, and toes,
Knees and toes.
Head, shoulders, knees, and toes,
Knees and toes.
Eyes and ears and mouth and nose.
Head and shoulders, knees and toes,
Knees and toes.

- It is fun to sing this song faster and faster.
- Sing the song again, substituting other parts of the body. The important thing to remember is to sing them in the same order.

105

Going to the Market

Teaches memory skills

- This game helps improve children's short-term memory. They will have to remember several words in the correct order.
- Say this poem:

  Susie went to the market. Susie went to the store.
  But when Susie got there, she forgot what she went for.
  Mama gave her a list. Mama gave it to her twice.
  And what Mama wanted was a big box of rice...

- Ask, "What did Mama want?" The children say, "A box of rice."
- Now say, "Mama wanted a box of *rice and bananas*." The children repeat what you said.
- Keep adding words. Start with three or four words and add more as children get more proficient.
- Once they can do this well, play the same game but emphasize a letter sound. Start all the words with the same letter, such as "horse," "haircut," and "honey."

Sequencing Sounds

Teaches auditory discrimination

Group Game

- Put four or five rhythm instruments in front of you.
- Play each one and talk about the sound. Talk about if it is high, low, tinkley, bell-like, and so on.
- Ask the children to close their eyes as you play one of the instruments. Then ask them to identify which one you played.
- Tell the children that you are going to play three instruments in a row, and that they should close their eyes and listen.
- After you have played three instruments, ask if someone can come to the front and play the instruments in the same order that you played them.
- Now let a child play three instruments and choose another child to come to the front and copy the sequence.

Another Sound Sequence Game

Teaches ordinal terms, such as first, second, third, middle, and last

Group Game

- Use the following sounds for this game—blowing a whistle, opening a window, ringing a bell, clapping, coughing, snapping fingers, hammering, pouring liquid, and noisy chewing.
- Pick three sounds and make them for the children.
- Now ask them to cover their eyes as they listen to the same sounds and try to identify them.
- Once the children have caught on to the game, make two noises, one after the other. Without peeking, the children are to guess the two sounds in sequence saying, "There were two sounds. First we heard a ____, and then we heard a ____."
- Continue the game and add three noises to listen for and tell the order.

Two-Part Stories

Teaches visualization

- Good readers see pictures in their heads as they read. To help children develop this skill, tell a story with two parts.
- After each part, ask a child to close her eyes and try to see a picture about the story.
- If the first part of the story is: "I walked with my dog to the bakery." ask her to try to see a picture of her walking with her dog. Help her describe the picture. "Where are you walking? Are you walking on the grass? Are you walking on the sidewalk?"
- For the second part of the story, ask her to close her eyes and try to see the bakery. Let her describe what she sees in the bakery.
- As children improve at this game, make it a three- or a four-part story.

Writing a Letter

Teaches about logical order

- Talk about the steps involved in writing a letter. To write a letter, you need to
  - get paper,
  - get a pencil,
  - write on the paper,
  - fold the paper,
  - put the paper into an envelope,
  - address the envelope,
  - seal the envelope,
  - put a stamp on the envelope, and
  - take it to the mailbox.
- Do each of these steps, creating a letter with the children. The letter can be one or two words, or even just a child's name.
- Send the letter to a friend, grandparents, or to the child.

Sight Word Games

8

What exactly are "sight words?" These are words that good readers may instantly recognize without having to "figure them out." Reading sight words builds the confidence of beginning readers and improves children's reading fluency.

A Word Wall is a list of sight words, or a systematically organized collection of words displayed in large letters on a wall or other large display place. A Word Wall is a tool to use, not just display. Word Walls are useful tools for individual learners, but work best to promote group learning.

Word Walls:

- support the teaching of important general principles about words and how they work.
- foster reading and writing.
- provide reference support for children during their reading and writing.
- promote children's independence as they work with words in writing and reading.
- provide a visual map to help children remember connections between words and characteristics that will help them form categories.
- develop a growing core of words that become part of a reading and writing vocabulary.

Word Wall Guidelines:

- Add words gradually.
- Make words very accessible by putting them where children can see them, writing them in big black letters, and using a variety of background colors so that the most often-confused words (there, their; what, when) are in different colors.
- Be selective about what words go on the wall, limiting additions to very common words that children use often in reading and writing.
- Practice those words by chanting and writing them.
- Do a variety of review activities to provide enough practice so children can read and spell words instantly and automatically.
- Make sure that children spell Word Wall words when they use the words in any writing that they do.
- Use upper- and lowercase letters appropriately, capitalizing only proper nouns.

How to Learn New Words

Teaches creativity

- Learn new words in a variety of ways, including:
  - See the words.
  - Say the words.
  - Chant the words (snap, clap, stomp, cheer).
  - Write the words.
  - Trace around the words with a red crayon.

Mind Reading

Teaches cognitive skills

- Think of a word on the wall and then give clues about that word.
- See if a child can "read your mind" and figure out which word you are talking about.
- The clues should follow like this:

  It's one of the words on the Word Wall.

  It has four letters.

  It begins with the letter ___.

  It ends with the letter ___.

- When the child figures out the word, he will be very excited.
- Suggest that he use that word in a sentence.

Flash the Word

Teaches concentration

Group Game

- Turn off the lights in the room.
- Take the flashlight and point it to a certain word on the Word Wall.
- Ask a child to read the word. (Choose words that you are sure he knows.)
- Now the child can shine the flashlight on the Word Wall and call on another child to read the word.

Word Wall Rhymes

Teaches cognitive skills

- Say a sentence that contains a word that rhymes with one of the Word Wall words and is spelled with the same pattern.
- The children find which Word Wall word rhymes, and how to spell it. For example, say, "The word begins with 'B' and rhymes with 'cat.'" The children say, "bat."
- Say, "The word begins with 'M' and rhymes with 'house.'" The children say, "mouse."
- Continue for as many as five words.
- This is a very exciting game for young children and really develops their reading skills.

Word Wall Sentences

Teaches sequencing skills

- Say a sentence using three or four of the Word Wall words.
- Repeat the sentence several times.
- Ask a child to point to each word in the sentence as you say it.
- Say another sentence and make it a little longer. Continue by repeating a sentence and then letting a child point to the words.
- Help children make up a sentence using the words on the Word Wall.

Tapping Out Words

Teaches segmenting skills

Group Game

- Select a word from the Word Wall.
- Say the word, then tap with a pencil, ruler, or pointer and say several letters in that word but not the whole word. Say, "Come. 'C,' 'O'…"
- Ask a child to finish spelling the word out loud: "'M,' 'E.'"
- When the child finishes spelling the word, that child calls out a new word, taps and spells part of the word, and calls on another child to finish.

Word Wall Cheer

Teaches spelling skills

- Choose five words from the Word Wall.
- Select one of the five words, and print each letter boldly on a separate piece of paper.
- Children ("cheerleaders") face the group, holding the letter papers to spell the word.
- Call out the first letter of the word. The child holding that letter steps forward and raises the letter paper as the other children say the letter.
- Continue until the entire word has been spelled.
- Say the word three times in unison.
- Take turns being cheerleaders and spelling the rest of the words.

Word Wall Chain

Teaches about beginning and ending sounds

Group Game

- Give each child five strips of construction paper. Use a variety of colors.
- The first child chooses any word from the Word Wall.
- All of the children write this word on one of their strips.
- The next child chooses another word that begins with the last letter of the previous word.
- Again, all of the children write the word on another strip of paper.
- Continue until all of the strips have words.
- Glue the strips together in the order that they were written and you have a Word Wall chain.

Word Wall Bingo

Teaches listening skills

Group Game

- Use tagboard or poster board to make a bingo card for each child. The card should have six blank spaces on it.
- Each child writes one Word Wall word in each space.
- In addition, all the words that are on the Word Wall are also on pieces of paper in a container.

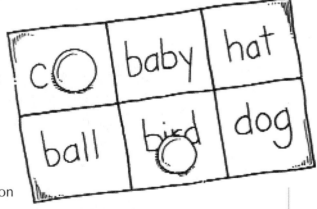

- One by one, pull a paper out of the container.
- Read the word and if that word is on a child's card, he can cover it with a place marker, such as a checker, bingo chip, or poker chip.
- When the entire card is covered, the child yells "Bingo."
- Play the game until everyone gets "Bingo" and all of the words have been used.

113

9

Story Play Games

Young children get ready for reading by being actively involved in stories. Read and tell stories to children every day. Encourage them to act out the stories that they have heard. Make time for children to tell their own stories, and talk about the stories they hear. Listen to what they say about the stories.

Young children can understand more than just the plot of a story. They are able to extend their thinking and discuss why events happened and why characters acted as they did. They can also make reasonable predictions about what will happen next and relate the story to events in their own lives. Being able to discuss stories they listen to now will help children interpret the meaning of stories when they are able to read independently.

Creative Storytelling

Teaches imagination

- Put a variety of familiar objects into a paper bag, such as keys, a book, a spoon, and a small toy. Tell the children they will use the objects to create a story.
- Remove the item from the bag one at a time, and every time you take an item out of the bag, make up a sentence about the item.
- For example: "Once upon a time there were some keys on the floor (key). When I picked up the keys, I laid them on a book (book)."
- Model making up stories with props so the children will learn how to create their own.
- Continue making new sentences about the objects in the bag.

Suggestions for Reading Books

Teaches a love of books

- Reading a book is not only enjoyable for both adult and child, it also stimulates children's desire to read books by themselves.
- Show the children that the words you are reading are the text on the page. This seems obvious, but children often think you are making it up from the pictures. Let them know it's mostly the text that carries the meaning. Following the words with your finger is very helpful.
- Show the children the cover and title page. Announce the name of the author and illustrator. This shows them that real people wrote the story. It might inspire them to write a book of their own.
- Show the children that books start at the front, and go through to the end; that you read from top to bottom, and from left to right. Point out page numbers.
- Read aloud with enthusiasm. Be an actor! Do silly voices.
- Stop reading from time to time to ask questions about what might happen next.

Stories From Art

Teaches the concept of order

- Select several pictures from magazines. Choose pictures that have objects that are familiar to children, for example, kitchen appliances, food, animals, community helpers, cars, planes, and trains.
- Start with three pictures, for example, a toaster, bread, and a dog. Show them to a child and talk about what is in each picture.
- Make up a story that goes with the pictures. For example:

Sally (child's name) put a piece of bread in the toaster. It cooked too long and got burnt. When she took it out of the toaster, it was very hot and she dropped it on the floor. Rags (the dog) quickly ran over and started eating the toast.

- Once the story is finished, the child can draw pictures about the story.

Story Retelling

Teaches oral language skills

- Telling and retelling a story helps children understand how parts of a story are related.
- Pick a favorite book. Read the book together.
- Say that you are going to tell the story from memory without using the book.
- Show the children the book, and then put it away and retell the story with enthusiasm and expression. If appropriate, use props. For example, you could use mittens for "The Three Little Kittens."
- Talk about the beginning, the middle, and the end of the story.
- Show the children the book and then tell the story again from memory.
- Now ask them to tell you the story.
- Tell and retell this story over a period of several days.

Stories Come to Life

Teaches listening skills

- Reading is important, but creating and acting out a story makes it come to life and helps children internalize the concepts in the story.
- Read a story that children know. Read the story, and as you read, find one word such as "run," and say it in a loud voice.
- Ask a child to act out the "loud" word when she hears it (by running).
- Also use words that show emotion such as "happy" and "sad," and ask children to act out those emotions.

Tic Tac Toe Story

Teaches comprehension skills

- Choose a book that a child loves.
- After reading the story, make a Tic Tac Toe diagram on a piece of paper.
- Ask the child questions about the story. If she knows the answer, she makes an "X" on the paper.
- If she does not know the answer, put an O on the paper.
- The object is to get three "X's" in a row.

What's on the Page?

Teaches cognitive skills

- You will need a book that has pictures on each page, and a piece of paper to cover the pictures.
- Choose an interesting story with colorful pictures.
- Cover the picture on the first page and then read it to a child.
- Stop reading at the end of the page and ask him to tell you what the page was about.
- Now ask him to guess what the picture will be on the page.
- Show the picture and talk about it. Then go to the next page and play the game again.

Listening for Differences

Teaches listening skills

- This game helps children hear differences between what they expect to hear and what they actually hear.
- Play this game by reciting nursery rhymes or poems that children know.
- Invite a child to sit down and close her eyes so that she can concentrate on what she will hear.
- Recite or read a familiar story or poem to the children. Their challenge is to detect changes whenever they occur.
- Then change the words. For example, say, "Dumpty Humpty sat on the wall," or "Jill and Jack went up the hill."
- You can also substitute words: "Little Boy Purple come blow your horn," or change the word order: "The bus on the wheels go 'round and 'round," or switch the order of events. Tell the story of "Little Red Riding Hood" and have her go to Grandma's house before she goes through the woods.
- At first, make the changes obvious.
- This game will develop good listening skills.
- Here are some more ideas:
  - "Twinkle, twinkle, little jar."
  - "Humpty Dumpty wall on a sat."
  - "One, two, shuckle my boo."
  - "Little Miss Muffet, eating her tuffet, sat on her curds and whey."
  - "Goldilocks went into the house and knocked on the door."
  - "Old Mother Hubbard, went to the cupboard to get her poor bone a dog."
  - "Hickory dickory dock, the clock went up the mouse."

Fun Games With a Book

Teaches a joy of reading

- Reading books presents many opportunities for developing children's reading skills.
- If the story has rhyming words, stop and let them guess the rhyming word.
- If the story has recurring words or phrases, stop and let them fill in the words. For example, in "The Three Little Pigs," the children could fill in the recurring sentence, "I'll huff and I'll puff and I'll blow your house down."
- If the story has a predictable sentence, let them guess the end of the line. "Brown Bear, Brown Bear, what do you see? I see a flower _____ (looking at me)."
- All of these ideas will strengthen children's reading development.

A Together Story

Teaches creativity

- This activity is a wonderful opportunity to connect with children through stories.
- Find out the likes, dislikes, ideas, and interests of a child.
- Make up a story that features the child as the hero or central character of the story.
- For example, if the child loves animals, in the story she might be the director of a zoo. If the child's favorite book is a Clifford book, Clifford might make a special appearance in the story. If the child wants to be a doctor, the child in the story might be a doctor who finds a cure for giggling.
- Illustrate the story with the child.
- Bind the story to make a book that the child can enjoy again and again.
- Share the story with other friends and family.

Imaginative Stories

Teaches creativity

- Retell a familiar story and make up your own changes. For example, instead of "Goldilocks and the Three Bears," call the story "Goldilocks and the Three Billy Goats Gruff."
- Tell the story, but change the dialogue to sound like the billy goats. For example, "Who's been sleeping in my bed, trip trap, trip trap?"
- Improvise, using familiar stories. This develops a great love for stories and also develops children's imagination.

A Toy Adventure

Teaches imagination

- Take a favorite stuffed toy, such as a stuffed dog, and make up a story about it. If the toy has a name, use it in the story and also use the child's name. If the child's favorite stuffed animal is "Mickey," call the story "Mickey's Adventure."
- The story should mention familiar people, places, and things, such as going to the park, riding in the car, visiting Grandma, and so on.
- Then ask the child to make up a story about her favorite stuffed toy. Remember that she may copy your story and that is fine. She needs a point of reference to get started.

Comparing Characters

Teaches about similarities and differences

- Pick two stories that have the same character in the story, for example, the wolf in "The Three Little Pigs" and in "Little Red Riding Hood."
- Tell each story and talk about the wolf in each story. Discuss his personality, the way he looks, and other characteristics.
- Read each story and compare the pictures of the wolf in each book.
- Read two editions of the same story and compare the pictures.
- Let children act out each story.

The Story's End

Teaches imagination

- An important part of reading and listening to stories is learning that they have endings.
- Sometimes the end of a story is a surprise, and sometimes it is not. Once children become familiar with stories, they can help create their own ending to a story.
- Read several familiar stories to the children, and talk about their different endings.
- Read an unfamiliar story.
- When you get close to the end of the story, stop reading and ask the children how they would finish the story. Tell them they may end the story any way they want.
- Write down their suggestions for the story's ending.
- Finish reading the story and talk about how the story's ending and the children's endings are similar or different.
- As an extension, ask them to draw a picture about the ending and give them an opportunity to talk about their picture.

10

Word Games

Developing the ability to read a text accurately and quickly is called reading fluency. Children must learn to read words rapidly and accurately in order to understand what they read. When fluent readers read silently, they recognize words automatically. When fluent readers read aloud, they read effortlessly and with expression. Readers who are weak in fluency read slowly, word by word, focusing on decoding words instead of comprehending meaning.

Learning the meaning and pronunciation of words is called vocabulary development. Children need to actively build and expand their knowledge of written and spoken words, what they mean, and how they are used.

Magnetic Words

Teaches fine motor skills

- You will need assorted letter magnets, which are available at school supply stores and other retail stores.
- Put the letters on a large cookie sheet.
- Help a child spell different words with the magnetic letters.
- Help him arrange the letters in alphabetical order.

Color Book of Words

Teaches about how books are made

- Staple together 26 pages of white paper.
- Working together with a child, put one letter on each page with a different colored crayon or marker.
- Each time a child discovers a new word in a book or magazine, help him put the word on the page of its beginning letter. Also, use the same color crayon or marker for all the words on that page.
- Soon you will have a lovely book of words in many colors.

Rainbow Words

Teaches color recognition

- Practice writing words with colored markers.
- Start with names and make each letter a different color.
- Using primary colors first can lead to a discussion about mixing colors.
- After talking about mixing colors, try mixing colors while writing names.

Scrabble® Words

Teaches visual discrimination

- Take the letters from a Scrabble® set and practice making words on a flat surface.
- Start with the child's name. Let him find the letters and then make the word.
- If there are certain words that he wants to make, encourage him and help him find the letters for that word.
- Try making words that you can use immediately. For example, the word "walk." Make the word and then walk. This is wonderful for improving comprehension skills.

Making Real and Silly Words

Teaches vocabulary

- You will need three small containers. Margarine tubs work well for this.
- Take small pieces of paper and write one letter on each piece of paper. Put consonants in the first and third box, and vowels in the middle box. Be sure that the consonants are sounds that children know. Some suggestions for letters are: "A," "S," "T," "R," "E," "N," "I," and "G."
- Take a piece of paper from each box. Say the first consonant, the second vowel sound, and the third consonant sound. Say the sounds separately, and then together as a word.
- Ask the child, "Is this a real word or a silly word?"
- This game will help children make new words with sounds that they already know.

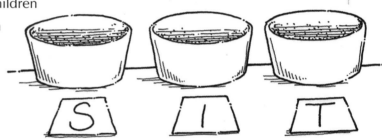

Letter Stepping

Teaches balance and coordination

- Print the letters of the alphabet on a large piece of butcher paper.
Note: For younger children, print the letters in alphabetical order; for children age six and older, print letters in random order.
- Tape it securely to the floor.
- Say a word to a child, and ask a child to step on each letter to spell it out. As he steps, he says the name of the letter.
- Start with the child's name.
- This is a lot of fun.

Author's Note: I played this with my grandson, who is six years old, and he could have played it for hours.

Alphabet Sentences

Teaches vocabulary

- Write down the first five letters of the alphabet, "A," "B," "C," "D," and "E."
- Ask a child to make up a sentence using words that start with letters in alphabetical order. If the child does not understand the concept of sentences, then just use words in that order.

  "A," "B," "C," "D,""E": Amy brings candy during exercise.

  "F," "G," "H," "I," "J": Find girls' hats in January.

- These can get pretty silly and that can be a lot of fun.
- Try the same game using the letters in your name or a child's name.

Making Up Sentences

Teaches comprehension

- This is a nice quiet game to play that reinforces comprehension.
- Look at pictures in a magazine. Find a picture that the child really likes, such as a picture of a dog.
- Point to it in the magazine.
- Talk with the child about the dog. Ask how big it is, what color fur it has, whether it's frisky, if it's having fun, and so on.
- Make up a sentence about the dog and then let the child make up a sentence.
- Cut out the dog picture and put it on some plain white paper with either glue or tape.
- Write the child's sentence next to the picture.

What Can I Do With _____?

Teaches imagination

- Pick a word that the children know and say the following rhyme:

What Can I Do With _____? by Jackie Silberg
What can I do with "cat"?
I can say it. (Say "cat.")
I can spell it. (Spell the word.)
I can act it. (Pretend to be a cat.)
And I can YELL it! (Yell the word.)
That's what I'll do with "cat."

- Choose another word and say the rhyme together with that word.

Comprehension Game

Teaches memory skills

- Make a list of action words for a child to do during the day. The words should have three or four letters. For example, the list could include "draw," "eat," "wash," and "skip."
- Write the words on a piece of paper or on a white board.
- Explain that throughout the day whenever he does one of the words, he should draw a line through the word. So, when he washes his hands, he can draw a line through the word "wash."
- Keep the list short and as his recognition of words improves, make it longer.

Pick a Word

Teaches listening skills

- Read a favorite story to a child.
- When reading the story, pick a special word in the story and say it in a different way each time you encounter it.
- For example, with the word "day," each time you come to it in the story, say it in a loud voice, a soft voice, a singing voice, and so on.
- Try to use the word "day" throughout the day and encourage the child to do the same.
- Children enjoy this game very much. After you have played it a few times, let the children pick out the word to emphasize.

Comparing Art and Words

Teaches imagination

- Show the child a picture of an animal, preferably a dog or a cat.
- Talk about how the picture looks like a dog and why we know it is a dog. The face, the legs, and the tail are all part of the dog.
- Do this with several different pictures, such as pictures of a man, a woman, a chair, a table, or any other familiar person or object. Talk about the whole picture and then the different parts of the picture that help us know what the picture is about.
- Here comes the fun. Tell the child that words are pictures too. It is possible to look at the whole word and at the parts of the word.
- Use the child's name as the first example because children recognize their name by the way it looks.
- Talk about the individual letters and sounds and show how the different parts make the word.
- This is a fascinating game and really helps conceptualize understanding words.

Song Title Words

Teaches listening skills

- Sing the first line of a familiar song and let the children fill in the last word.

  Note: Use the last word of the first line for three- and four-year-olds; with older children, you can make it more complicated.

- Write the word on a chalkboard, piece of paper, or white board.

- Also write the word on an index card and put it in a special box.

- Once the children are familiar with several of the words, ask children to pick an index card and identify the song by the word.

- Here are songs to start with.

  - "Twinkle, twinkle little _____." (star)
  - "The wheels on the bus go 'round and _____." ('round)
  - "Mary had a little _____." (lamb)
  - "Do you know the muffin _____?" (man)
  - "The itsy bitsy spider went up the water _____." (spout)
  - "This old man, he played ____." (one)

- There are many games that you can play with these words. Think of words from familiar songs that rhyme. For example, "horn" and "corn" from "Little Boy Blue."

- You can also sing the song using a rhyming word. This is very silly and the children enjoy it, for example, "Do you know the Muffin Can?"

A Poem for Me

Teaches rhyming skills

- Encourage the children to make up a poem about themselves.
- The poem should include their name, an adjective about them, a favorite number, and a favorite color. Rhyme the color word.
- For example:

  My name is Ryan, and I am happy.
  I like the number seven and the color blue,
  And I like to play with you.

- Another example:

  My name is Michael and I am funny.
  I like four and the color red,
  And I like to jump up and down in my bed.

Word Listening

Teaches listening skills

- Say a word with two parts (compound word) to a child, for example "sunshine."

Note: A compound word is a word made up of two smaller words, in this case, "sun" and "shine."

- Ask a child to repeat the word after you.
- Now say the first part of the word "sun" and let him fill in the second part of the word "shine."
- Do this with several words, such as "baseball," "raincoat," "motorcycle," and "cookbook."
- Make up a story using the words that you have been talking about. As you tell the story, only say the first part of the word.
- Hearing and saying the parts of words helps prepare children for reading.

Spelling Puzzles

Teaches cognitive skills

- Write familiar words on different colors of tag board.
- Cut the words apart in a variety of ways.
  - Put each individual word in a small zipper-closure bag.
  - Children put each puzzle back together to form the word.
  - When they discover the word, they can shout it out.

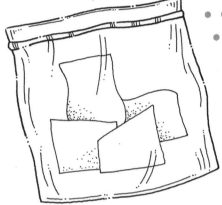
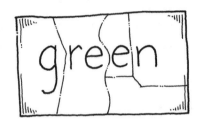

Puzzle Words

Teaches fine motor skills

- You will need index cards, envelopes, crayons, and scissors.
- Write simple words on index cards—"ball," "dog," "fish," and so on. Make about five cards and put each one in an envelope.
- On the outside of an envelope, draw or glue a picture that will match the word inside.
- Give a child an envelope and ask him to cut apart an index card with the word on it, letter by letter, using in a zigzag pattern to make puzzle pieces.
- Ask him to place the letters together while blending the phonemes aloud.
- Store the puzzle pieces in the matching envelopes.

Sorry

Teaches language skills

- On several index cards, write words that the children can read. Add one or two new words that they do not know.
- Write "Sorry" on a few cards. Place all the cards in a box.
- Ask a child to take out a card and say the word. If he knows the word, he can keep the card.
- If he draws the word "Sorry", he has to put all his words back in and start over.
- This is a fun game and really helps children learn words.

Acting Out Words

Teaches dramatic play skills

- Make a list of words that children recognize and write the words on pieces of paper or index cards, one word per card.
- Ask a child to select a card and tell you the word.
- Now ask him to act out the word.
- The words that you use should be nouns, such as "cat," "dog," "pig," and so on.

Photograph Words

Teaches memory skills

- Use photographs as a writing tool.
- Take photographs of street signs, store signs, mailbox numbers, "For Sale" signs, advertisements, bus stop signs, church names, and so on.
- After the photographs are printed, help the children paste them on a large piece of paper.
- Ask the children to say what they remember about the signs.
- Encourage them to add drawings to the paper.
- "Read" this entire "newspaper."

131

Word for the Day

Teaches vocabulary

- Select a special box to be a child's "word box."
- Each day he picks a word to add to his word box. Write the word for him on an index card.
- Prompt him to choose words by talking about family, neighbors, places to visit, playing with friends, and other familiar people and places.
- Encourage him to decorate his box with stickers and markers.

- Each day, review the old words before you add a new one.
- Children take pride in reading the words in their box.
- Pick three cards and try making up a story using the three words.

The Newspaper Game

Teaches observation skills

- You will need a newspaper or magazine, a colored marker or highlighter, scissors, a piece of paper, paste or glue, and a blank piece of paper.
- Pick a page in the newspaper. Circle or highlight words on the page that a child can read.
- Tell the child, "Today, we're going to find words that you know, so that you can make your own newspaper of words on this sheet of paper."
- Say, "In this game, you read the words I've marked. After you read each one, cut it out and glue it onto this blank piece of paper."
- Each day, add more words to the paper. Soon the children will have a full page of newpaper words that they know.

Word Family Game

Teaches explanation of sound

- Make a series of sentence strips with a word family on each (the end sound of a word, minus the beginning consonant). Some ideas are: "ike," "at," "eg," "og," illy," and so on.
- Make separate sentence strips with a consonant on each strip.
- Give a child a sentence strip with "ike." Ask him to find a letter to put at the beginning.
- Ask him to read the word. It can be a real or a silly word. With "ike" you might make "hike," "like," "pike," "zike," "bike," and so on.
- Remember to point out that the last letters of each word are the same.

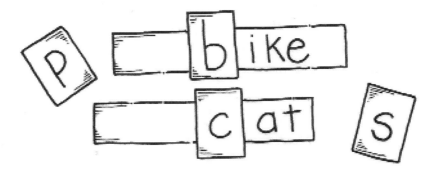

What's the Word?

Teaches recognizing letter sounds

- Write consonants on 3 x 5 index cards and families of words on others, for example, "at," "ig," "ite," and then many consonants.
- Put the word families and the consonants into separate boxes.
- Let a child pick a card from each box. Ask him to put the cards together to see if they make a word.
- He will sound out the letters on each card and say the word.
- Make this game more challenging by using consonant blends, such as "tr" or "st."

What's the Object?

Teaches observation skills

- Choose a familiar object in the room and don't tell the children which object you have chosen.
- Say the name of the object, substituting the first letter of the word you have chosen with another consonant sound that the children know. For example, instead of saying the word "table" say the word "wable."
- After saying this new word, ask the children to guess what object you are talking about.
- If they answer correctly, ask them to say another word using the letter you inserted in the beginning of the word. Using the example above, they could say **w**ood, **w**ater, or **w**and.

Sound Walk

Teaches phonemic awareness and listening skills

- Take a "sound walk." Remind everyone that they need to be very quiet in order to hear all the different sounds.
- Establish a purpose for the listening. Ask the children to listen and see how many different sounds they can hear, and see if they can tell who or what is making each sound.
- Continue by listening for and trying to remember the **softest or quietest sound** and/or the **loudest sound** they heard.
- Listen for the **first sound** that they hear after your signal to begin.
- Ask them to notice, and try to remember, the **last sound** they heard before you signaled that the listening part of the walk was over. Listening for first and last sounds helps develop phonemic awareness.
- When the walk is over, talk about the sounds and write down the names of the things that made the sounds.
- Practice reading the new words that you have learned.

Nursery Rhyme Words

Teaches imagination

- Many nursery rhyme words are unusual and need to be explained to young children. One nursery rhyme you might want to use to introduce new words is "Little Miss Muffet."

  Little Miss Muffet sat on a tuffet
  Eating her curds and whey.
  Along came a spider and sat down beside her,
  And frightened Miss Muffet away.

- Talk about the words "tuffet," "curds," and "whey."
- This is a great story to act out. One child is Miss Muffet and another child is the spider. (You could also have a Mr. Muffet.) Miss Muffet sits down (on her "tuffet") and the spider comes and sits next to her.
- Ask the children what other things Miss Muffet and the spider could do together instead of Miss Muffet being frightened and running away. For example, they could talk about school, sing a song, or play a game.
- Acting out the words will help children internalize the meaning.
- You can also use the words "tuffet," "curds," and "whey" to talk about beginning sounds.

What Can You Tell Me?

Teaches observation skills and vocabulary

Group Game

- This is a very effective group game for developing vocabulary.
- Give one child an object. Have him look at it and tell you one thing about it. For example, if the object is a ball, the child could tell the shape, the color, how it feels, and so on.
- He passes it on to the next child who tells one more thing about the object, and then passes it to the next child until the children have exhausted ways to describe the object.
- Write the word (in this case "ball"), and under it, write all of the description words that were used.
- You can also add these words to a sight word chart or Word Wall.

Word Rhythms

Teaches listening skills

- Listening to the rhythm of words is an important reading skill.
- Say your name to a child, for example, "Jackie."
- Say a child's name, for example, "Michael," and ask the child if the two names have the same number of syllables.
- Look around the room and name other words with two syllables and compare them to your names.
- Now find a word with more than two syllables, for example, "banana," and ask if that word has the same number of syllables.
- Comparing the syllables takes a lot of listening and thinking. Remember that these are rhythmic sounds and not phonemic sounds.

Label Matching

Teaches about sight words

- Collect household product boxes (two of each).
- Cut the labels from each box (laundry detergents, toothpaste, cereal, and so on).
- Try to cut the labels as close to the same size as possible.
- Mix all the labels together, and then ask a child to match two words from the labels that are the same.

- Talk about the word, the beginning letter, and the sound that it makes.

Familiar Words

Teaches observation skills

- There are so many words that children see on a regular basis that provide important information. These signs include "exit" and "enter" signs, traffic signs, room signs at school, and, of course, fast food signs.
- Go on a stroll and each time you see a sign, identify it, say the word, and write it down in a notebook (or help the children write it down).
- When you get back, write the words on the chalkboard or white board and review with the children.
- Repeat this on another day. It is a wonderful way to develop a reading vocabulary.

11

Writing Games

Children can learn reading skills by connecting real-life experiences with literacy. You can use writing every day. For example, graph children's height, list children's names by birthday, write the directions for doing a dance, write the words of songs, write vegetable and flower names on stakes to put in the garden, and so on.

Sand Writing

Teaches creativity

- Give a child a box partially filled with sand or salt. Shoeboxes work well.
- Include some interesting writing utensils in the box, such as unsharpened pencils, plastic spoons, or crayons.
- Let the child draw a letter in the sand. Start with the beginning letter of her name.
- Once she starts, she will have great fun erasing the letter and writing another one.
- Experiment with different writing tools to create letters of different sizes and shapes.

Disappearing Letters

Teaches eye-hand coordination

- You will need a chalkboard, paintbrushes, and a container of water.
- Using chalk, write a letter on the chalkboard.
- Ask a child to dip a paintbrush into the water and trace the letter on the chalkboard.
- As she paints over it, it will disappear.
- You can also do this with shapes and numbers.

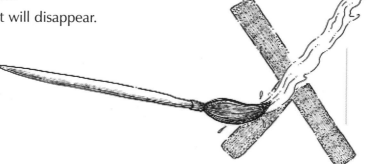

Making Letters

Teaches cognitive thinking

- Sit down with a child and let her select the crayon of her choice.
- Draw a vertical line on a piece of paper.
- Suggest ways to turn that line into a letter. If necessary, give some choices, such as an "I," "T," "D," and so on.
- Keep playing this game by drawing other parts of letters, such as curves, horizontal lines, or slanted lines. If necessary, always give the child suggestions as to what letters to make.

Flashlight Letters

Teaches observation skills and letter recognition

- Darken the room. With a flashlight, make a letter on the ceiling.
- As a child watches you do this, see if she can identify the letter.
- Give the flashlight to her and let her write a letter on the ceiling.

Tissue Paper Tracing

Teaches eye-hand coordination

- Print a child's name on a large piece of paper.
- Give the child a piece of tracing paper to cover the letters.
- Show her how to trace over the letters with a large crayon.
- Start with just one letter and add others as she becomes more confident.

Making Cereal and Cracker Letters

Teaches coordination

- Give children a plate or paper towel and an assortment of round, dry cereal (such as Cheerios) and small, straight crackers.
- Encourage the children to use the round cereal and the straight crackers (breaking them into pieces if necessary) to make edible names and words.
- After they are finished, they can eat their words!

Ways to Write Names

Teaches about art media

- Provide an assortment of the following materials so children can practice writing, forming, and decorating their names:
  - pencils and a variety of papers
  - crayons and a variety of papers
  - markers and a variety of papers
  - playdough or clay and a cutting board
  - Wikki Stix® and paper
  - finger paints and paper
  - chalk and chalkboards
  - chalk on the sidewalk
  - paintbrush and water on the sidewalk
  - white glue on black paper, with or without glitter, seeds, or yarn
  - shaving cream on a tabletop
  - Tinkertoys® and other building toys
  - pipe cleaners / chenille craft stems
- Ask the children for their ideas!

Crayon Resist Names

Teaches fine motor skills

- Ask a child to write her name three times with crayon on a piece of white construction paper.
- Encourage her to press firmly with the crayon to make a deep, rich color.
- Ask her to trace over the letters that she has written.
- Give her watercolor paint to paint over the entire page. Blue or black is the most effective.
- Set the picture aside to dry.
- The watercolor is absorbed by the paper and resisted by the crayon markings.
- This is a very attractive work of art to display.
- You can decorate the picture with glitter and sequins.

Name Practice

Teaches fine motor skills

- This is a helpful activity for practicing writing names and tracing.
- Fold a sheet of white paper (8 ½ x 11) into thirds vertically. There will be a top flap and a bottom flap that will fold over the middle section.
- Open the paper up, and in the middle section write the child's name with a broad-tipped black marker.
- Show the children how to fold the top flap down over their name and practice tracing their name using a pencil or crayon.
- When they have finished, they fold the top flap up again.
- Now fold the bottom flap up and over their name and trace their name again.
- When finished tracing, the two flaps can be folded backwards, and it will form a name plate showing the name written in marker.

Three Pigs List

Teaches about making lists

- Read the story of "The Three Little Pigs."
- Talk about the story with the children and make a "To Do" list of things the pigs need to build their homes.
- As you decide what should be on the list, write the beginning letter of each word and ask the children to make its sound.
- Then, write the word in black marker and give the children paper to trace over the letters.
- Some things on your list might be bricks, sticks, or straw. The version of your story will be your guide.
- There are many stories that fit this game. Think of the ones that are familiar to the children.

Menu Writing

Teaches about nutrition

Group Game

- Making up menus is fun and will give children practice in writing.
- Plan a menu that consists of healthy and nutritional foods.
- Divide it into three parts—appetizer, main course, and dessert.
- As you discuss the food, write down the words. Let one child write the first letter of each food.
- Plan a meal and then prepare it with the children.
- Present the menu before serving the meal.

Happy Birthday

Teaches vocabulary

Group Game

- Sing "Happy Birthday" to the birthday child.
- Write the word "happy" on a large piece of paper or on the chalkboard.
- Ask the children what makes them happy.
- As each child answers, turn his answer into one word. For example, if a child says, "My dog makes me happy." Write the word "dog" on the paper.
- Continue as long as the children are interested.
- Let the children copy the words on their own paper, creating "happy" papers. They can add to their paper with pictures and stickers.

The Calendar Game

Teaches organization skills

- On an 8 ½ x 11 piece of paper, create a calendar for a week. Make one for yourself and one for the children.
- Point out the names of each day at the top of the paper (see example).
- Divide each day into morning, afternoon, and evening.
- Talk about the things that you do each day, such as nap, play, eat meals, and take a bath. Write these words on the calendar at the appropriate time of day.
- Let the child copy the words that you write. If she cannot, let her draw a picture or use an appropriate sticker.
- Look at the calendar each day and talk about what will happen during the day.
- Don't forget to put special events, such as birthdays or trips, on the calendar.

	Sun.	Mon.	Tue.	Wed.	Thu.	Fri.	Sat.
morning	eat	play					
afternoon	play	nap					
evening	bed	bath					

Appendix

Glossary

Alliteration is the repetition of initial consonant sounds in two or more neighboring words or syllables.

The **Alphabet** is a set of letters, characters, or symbols that indicate letters or speech sounds. An alphabet is often arranged in a customary order, for example, the English alphabet has the following order: a b c d e f g h i j k l m n o p q r s t u v w x y z.

Blending is the process of forming a word by combining parts of words. In blending you sound out a sound or phoneme and combine it with the next sound or phoneme of the same word. Eventually, all sounds or phonemes of a word form the word itself. Blending is used in the phonics approach to teaching reading. Examples of blending include the sounds /b/ /a/ /t/ become the word "bat" and the syllables /ba/ /na/ /na/ make the word "banana."

Comprehension is the ability to grasp something mentally and the capacity to understand ideas and facts. Reading requires understanding, or comprehending, the meaning of print.

Decoding Skills are the skills necessary to analyze and interpret correctly the spoken or graphic symbols of a familiar language. They are also known as word attack skills.

Graphemes are the 26 letters of the alphabet.

Graphophonic is one of the cueing systems that help children understand an unknown word in a text. It refers to how a letter looks and sounds.

High Frequency Words are words repeated frequently in a story or song.

Invented Spelling refers to the practice of allowing or encouraging beginning readers to write any way they want. The idea is that the act of writing, for the beginner, is more important than correctness of form (correct spelling). Eventually, according to this school of thought, children will learn and use the correct form. Allowing the use of invented spelling encourages learners to produce their own creative writing patterns, and write and experiment with letters and shapes without being expected to follow conventional rules.

Literacy is the quality or state of being able to read and write.

A **Phoneme** is a member of the set of the smallest units of speech that serve to distinguish one sound from another in a language or dialect. There are 44 sounds, or phonemes, that make up English words. A unit of speech is considered a phoneme if replacing it in a word results in a change of meaning, for example, "**p**in" becomes "**b**in," "**b**at" becomes "**r**at," and "c**o**t" becomes "c**u**t."

Phonemic Awareness is the ability to recognize that a spoken word consists of "a sequence of individual sounds" (Ball and Blachman, 1991) and to "manipulate individual sounds in the speech stream" (Yopp, 1988).

Phonemic Awareness Skills are the skills needed to recognize that a spoken word consists of a sequence of individual sounds. These skills include segmentation, which is the ability to determine if two words start the same or end the same, to remove a phoneme from a word, to count phonemes in a word, and to blend sounds together. Another phonemic awareness skill is sound/symbol identification, which includes knowing letters by sight and by sound, and matching letters with the appropriate sounds, and vice versa.

Phonics is a method of teaching beginners to read and pronounce words by learning to associate letters or letter groups with the sounds they represent.

Segmentation is the ability to isolate sounds from a stream of speech.

Shared Reading is a reading activity where an adult reads a story while a child or a group of children look at the text being read and follow along.

A **Sight Word** is a word that good readers recognize and know without having to "figure it out."

A **Syllable** is a unit of sound minimally composed of a vowel, but with optional beginning and ending consonants.

Whole Language is a reading strategy where the "language is kept whole, not fragmented into skills; literacy skills and strategies are developed in the context of whole, authentic literacy events, while reading and writing experiences permeate the whole curriculum; and learning within the classroom is integrated with the whole life of the learner" (Weaver 1990).

About Books

Books are an essential part of learning to read. They encourage children to form their own pictures in their minds, stimulating imagination. They are a shared experience between reader and listener. They invite children to repeat and practice language. Unlike a television program, which is momentary, books are permanent objects that can be enjoyed repeatedly.

Book List

The list below is a beginning book list. For additional ideas and suggestions, talk to teachers, friends, children's librarians, or experts at children's bookstores or children's departments in large bookstores. Take children to the library and to bookstores and let them look through books and pick out the ones that they want to read.

100 Knock Knock Jokes for Kids by Michael Kilgarriff
All About Arthur: An Absolutely Absurd Ape by Eric Carle
Alligator Pie by Dennis Lee
Alligators All Around: An Alphabet by Maurice Sendak
Amelia Bedelia books by Peggy Parrish
Animalia by Graeme Base
Dinosaur Chase by Carolyn Otto
Frogs in Clogs by Sheila White Samton
Green Eggs and Ham by Dr. Seuss
Hush, Little Baby by Margot Zemach
Is Your Mama a Llama? by Deborah Guarino and Steven Kellogg
Jelly Belly: Original Nursery Rhymes by Dennis Lee
Moose on the Loose by Carol Patridge Ochs
Mrs. Wishy Washy by Joy Cowley
My Parents Think I'm Sleeping by Jack Prelutsky
There's a Wocket in My Pocket by Dr. Seuss
When We Were Very Young by A.A. Milne
Where the Sidewalk Ends by Shel Silverstein
Zin! Zin! Zin! A Violin by Lloyd Moss

For more book suggestions, ask teachers and parents, or consider the following websites and organizations:
- Reading Rockets, www.readingrockets.com
- American Library Association, www.ala.org
- Children's Round Table, a unit of the Texas Library Association, Austin, www.txtla.org/groups/crt
- Reading Is Fundamental, www.rif.org

Reading Milestones

Reading Milestones for Preschoolers*

By age four, most preschoolers are able to:
- Understand complicated language
- Enjoy listening to complex stories
- Recognize and have fun with rhymes
- Participate in focused conversations
- Narrate actions with words
- Use creative language
- Recognize some familiar words
- Learn that stories have a clear structure and specific elements
- "Pretend" to read
- Recognize print in everyday life, on cereal boxes, street signs, and more
- Know that print is used for many different purposes, from stories to grocery lists
- Learn to hold a book, turn the pages, and pretend to read
- Ask questions and make comments that show they understand what you are reading to them
- Sing the ABC song
- Recognize the shape of letters
- Begin to make real letters
- Ask for help in learning to write letters
- Begin to show interest in what adults write, such as a grocery list or a thank-you note
- Know some of the alphabet sounds, and may be able to recognize matching sounds and some printed letters and numbers
- Understand ideas such as beside, above, under, near, and far
- Listen, follow directions, and focus on a specific task
- Take turns speaking in a conversation
- Begin to understand the connection between spoken and written words
- Count, sort, compare, and know shapes
- Hold a pencil or crayon the correct way
- "Write" ideas or notes by scribbling

* The Preschool Milestones were adapted from *Checkpoints for Progress in Reading and Writing for Families and Communities* and *Checkpoints for Progress in Reading and Writing for Teachers and Learning Partners* (February 1998) (http://www.ed.gov/pubs/CheckFamilies/birth-36.html).
These booklets provide developmental milestones for children from birth through grade 12 and explain what most children are able to read and write within these periods. They are free and available online at the website address above or by calling 1-877-4ED-PUBS.

Kindergarten Milestones*

By age five, most kindergartners are able to:
- Sound like they are reading when pretending to read
- Enjoy being read to, have favorite books, and retell simple stories
- Use descriptive language to explain or to ask questions
- Recognize letters and letter-sound correspondence
- Show familiarity with rhyming and beginning sounds
- Understand that (English) print is read left to right and top to bottom
- Begin to match spoken words with written ones
- Begin to write letters of the alphabet and some words they use and hear often
- Begin to write stories with some readable parts
- Know the letters and sounds of the alphabet
- Know simple words like "the," "and," "it," and "is"
- Start to read signs, food packages, and other everyday items
- Use scribbling, pictures, and some letters and words to tell a story
- Begin to use letters and sounds they know to start writing things such as lists and invitations
- Develop their memory for things they hear
- Frequently ask questions about words and concepts they do not understand
- Understand complicated sentences
- Listen to lengthy stories
- Begin to realize that they are writers
- Use invented spelling
- Write some words the "right" way
- Read what they have written
- Tell a complete story about something that interests them
- Explain how to do simple tasks
- Develop an awareness of sounds and words
- Learn the rules of conversation

*The Kindergarten Milestones were adapted from *Helping Your Child Become a Reader*, U.S. Department of Education, Office of Educational Research and Improvement (January 2000).

Reading Milestones for Six-Year-Olds*

By age six, most children are able to:
- Talk about their experiences, including many details
- Know thousands of words
- Love to talk about the books they read and listen to
- Have speaking that is more rich and complex than their writing
- Are learning to "crack the code" of the written word
- Know many words by sight
- Read simple books smoothly, but generally read word by word
- Detect their reading mistakes
- Revise their writing
- Use a combination of "invented" and correct spelling
- Write many times a day for different purposes
- Use only some punctuation
- Use "story language" in their own writing
- Enjoy listening to long stories
- Learn new word meanings through listening and talking
- Learn how to be a good listener

*The Kindergarten Milestones and Reading Milestones for Six-Year-Olds were adapted from *Helping Your Child Become a Reader*, U.S. Department of Education, Office of Educational Research and Improvement, January 2000.

Bibliography

Adams, M. J. (1990). *Beginning to read: Thinking and learning about print*. Cambridge, MA: Bolt, Beranek, and Newman, Inc. [ED 317 950]

Backman, J. E. (1983). Psycholinguistic skills and reading acquisition: A look at early readers. *Reading Research Quarterly*, 18, 466-479.

Bradley, L. & P. E. Bryant. (1983). Categorizing sounds and learning to read—A causal connection. *Nature*, 301, 419-421.

Bruce, D. J. (1964). The analysis of word sounds by young children. *British Journal of Educational Psychology*, 34, 158-170.

Clay, M. (1991). *Becoming literate: The construction of inner control*. Portsmouth, NH: Heinemann.

Cunningham, A. E. (1989). Phonemic awareness: The development of early reading competency. *Reading Research Quarterly*, 24, 471-472.

Griffith, P. & M. W. Olson. (1992). Phonemic awareness helps beginning readers break the code. *Reading Teacher*, 45(7), 516-23. [EJ 439 120]

Hall, S. & L. Moats. (1998). *Straight talk about reading*. New York: McGraw-Hill.

Honig, B. (1996). *Teaching our children to read: The role of skills in a comprehensive reading program*. Thousand Oaks, CA: Corwin Press. [CS 012 479]

The Learning First Alliance. (2002). *Every child reading: A professional development guide*. Baltimore, MD: The Association for Supervision and Curriculum Development.

Lewkowicz, N. K. (1980). Phonemic awareness training: What to teach and how to teach it. *Journal of Educational Psychology*, 72, 686-700.

Lundberg, I., J. Frost, & O. Petersen. (1988). Effects of an extensive program for stimulating phonological awareness in preschool children. *Reading Research Quarterly*, 23, 263-284.

Lyon, G. R. (1997). Toward a definition of dyslexia. *Annals of Dyslexia*, 45, 3-27.

Reiben, L. & C. Perfetti. (1991). *Learning to read*. Hillsdale, NJ: Lawrence Erlbaum Associates.

Rozin, P., B. Bressman, & M. Taft. (1974). Do children understand the basic relationship between speech and writing? The Mow-Motorcycle test. *Journal of Reading Behavior, 6,* 327-334.

Schickedanz, J.A. (1999). *Much more than the ABC'S: The early stages of reading and writing.* Washington, DC: National Association for the Education of Young Children.

Share, D. L., A. F. Jorm, R. Maclean & R. Matthews. (1984). Sources of individual differences in reading acquisition. *Journal of Educational Psychology, 76,* 1309-1324.

Shaywitz, S. (1996). Dyslexia. *Scientific American,* November, 98-104.

Stanovich, K. E., Cunningham, A. E., & B. R. Cramer. (1984). Assessing phonological awareness in kindergarten children: Issues of task comparability. *Journal of Experimental Child Psychology, 38,* 175-190.

Tarasoff, M. (1993). *Reading instruction that makes sense.* Winnipeg, Manitoba, Canada: Portage and Main.

Yopp, H. K. (1988). The validity and reliability of phonemic awareness tests. *Reading Research Quarterly, 23,* 159-177.

Online Resources

www.acs.ucalgary.ca/~dkbrown/ (a children's literature web guide)
www.naeyc.org
www.reachoutandread.org
www.Readingrockets.com

Index